Tartarian E
Or
Millennial Kingdom?

Tartarian Rule?
Or
Millennial Kingdom?

Allan Cornford

Table of Contents

Introduction

Most of what we "know" today about our world, is based upon unproven theories such as evolution, the big bang, heliocentricity, the spinning globe model and gravity, which became generally accepted over the last few centuries. Upon these theories further assumptions have been made, each of them being refined over time. But each of these assumptions is based on the idea that all of the original theories are indeed factual.

When freeing oneself from a lifetime of indoctrination, the big bang, evolution, and the heliocentric globe model theory become a distant memory, a thing of the past. For on deeper reflection none of these theories add up, and we start to realize that many of the questions we had as a child were never fully answered. We just stopped asking the right questions.

To a degree the same is true with world history. I'm not saying history is based upon theory, or not in the main anyway. But time and again, anomalies crop up in the historical timeline which go unanswered in the official narrative. Where an answer of sorts is provided, it often raises further questions, or seems at odds with the time period the event supposedly occurred in.

It's all too easy to make sweeping generalizations without any hard evidence to back them up. History remains in the past, and now it's gone. What we are dealing with here, is the official narrative, which is a very powerful entity. Not only that, we only have visual evidence dating back to the 1840's. Hence any alternative view of history depends upon locating the anomalies, joining the dots, and using our imagination.

Likewise, unless we can say with all honesty, that our personal understanding of the timing of the rapture, or the millennial reign of Jesus Christ etc. is 100% accurate, then effectively, everything remains a theory.

The main theme of this book should also be considered a theory, an hypothesis, but what if this theory makes perfect sense? Whilst many might disagree entirely, how about those who might intuitively feel that it is all essentially true?

I'm not trying to prove anything, but would encourage others to think for themselves, because there is so much going on in this world that is not what it seems.

Around 18 months ago I began to notice a number of Facebook groups had emerged, with titles that included terms such as 'Tartaria', 'Old World Architecture' and 'Mud-flood' etc.

Suddenly everyone began looking at the grand architecture of their cities, and were discussing the possibility that these magnificent structures, which can be found in all cities across the entire world, could actually have been built long ago by a far more advanced civilization.

I was intrigued. So I watched a guy called Ewaranon's video presentation called "Lost History of the Flat Earth", and whilst I may not agree with everything he presented, I was completely blown away. It is one of the most impressive history lessons that I've ever had the privilege of witnessing. Completely understandable, but at the same time quite incredible.

The subject matter in question is like an enormous jigsaw puzzle, and this book will barely scratch the surface, and therefore give little justice to the subject in hand. Every piece of the giant jigsaw puzzle can be dissected, and an entire book written about it, so I will try to keep things about as general and basic as possible.

Before continuing, I'd like to clarify a couple of things. Although I've travelled extensively throughout the UK and have visited many cathedrals and other historic buildings over the years, I have only ventured from the shores of this "green and pleasant land" on two occasions in my entire life.

Where I refer to other nations it is not from first hand experience. Any knowledge I may seem to have of America for example, has been gleaned from listening to others, and my own personal research, primarily by way of the Internet.

Where I use the term "old world" (unless otherwise stated) it refers to an undisclosed and open-ended period of time, in perhaps the not too distant past.

Where I use the term "the controllers" I refer to a particular group of generally unknown, and unelected individuals, often referred to as the Cabal, the Elite or the Shadow Government. Some prefer to call them the Parasites.

By and large, *religion* as an institution, has been invented by the controllers of world history, and has been used as a weapon to control, to divide and to conquer. Religion has also been used with great success by the controllers, to justify the existence of the old world architecture and infrastructure.

It would seem that under the Sovereignty of Almighty God, the controllers operate unseen in the background on behalf of Satan, the god of this world. On the spiritual level, these wicked individuals are known as the *Archons*, a Greek word translated in the English language as, 'the principalities' in the Authorized King James Bible. The invisible powers, the rulers of the darkness of this world, who are at constant war with humanity. *(Ephesians 6:12.)*

They are the puppet masters, who from behind the veil, pull the strings of the kings of the earth. Those who work primarily through propaganda, fear and deception to manipulate the historical timeline and control world affairs.

Operating out of secrecy, the Cabal control all sides through a process which to the vast majority of folk might appear to be a natural one, but in reality it's a dialectic process, where the world is a stage and they pull the strings of the players on all sides.

On a human level and rooted in the ancient mystery schools, they are known as the Amalekites, devoid of empathy, who hate Jesus Christ with a passion, and have been at war with God from generation to generation.(*Exodus 17:16)*. They are also likely to be the same group of people, that Jesus referred to collectively as the Synagogue of Satan, and who are liars according to Jesus. *(Revelation 2;9 and Revelation 3:9.)*

Furthermore, Satan, the god they serve, is the god of this world, aeon or age, who has the ability to blind the minds of mankind. *(2 Corinthians 4.)* Not only is the god of this world a liar, he is also the father of the Lie. *(John 8:44.)* So if I were to suggest that we've been lied to and deceived about pretty much everything throughout our entire lives, it really should come as little or no surprise. For there's a very real sense by which, the odds have been stacked against us, from the moment we entered this world.

John 8:32. And ye shall know the truth, and the truth shall make you free.

John 8:36. If the Son therefore shall make you free, ye shall be free indeed.

Inheritance

In my two previous books, "The Kings of the Earth and the High Ones on High", and "The Needle or the Sword:An Alternative Worldview", I covered the original creation of the heavens and the earth *in the beginning*, and how the age, aeon or world that existed back in the heavens of old, was totally wiped out by a deluge on the scale of an Extinction Level Event. This left the earth ruined and barren, trapped in total darkness and submerged beneath the frozen surface waters of the great deep as described in Genesis 1:2. The first of the six days of *restoration* begins in verse 3 when God said 'Let there be light'.

The Bible indicates that the heavens and the earth *of old*, created by God *in the beginning*, were placed under the governance of Lucifer and the angels. In this pre-Adamic world, there existed gargantuan, silicon-based life forms, including trees, on a scale that literally went off the charts.

Following the ancient rebellion against God by Lucifer and his angelic cohorts, these gargantuan, towering trees were cut down, and during the catastrophic deluge which destroyed the prehistoric world, their massive stumps and root systems which remained in the ground, transitioned to stone in a natural process called petrification. The same petrification process was true for the gigantic Leviathan and Behemoth type creatures that formerly roamed the earth and inhabited its oceans.

2 Peter 3:5-7. For this they willingly are ignorant of, that by the word of God the heavens *were of old, and the earth* standing out of the water and in the water: Whereby *the world that then was*, being overflowed with water, perished: *But* the heavens and the earth, *which are now,* ....

Jeremiah 4:23. I beheld the earth, and, lo, *it was* without form, and void; and the heavens, and they *had* no light.

Genesis 1:2. And the earth was without form, and void; and darkness *was* upon the face of the deep. And the Spirit of God moved upon the face of the waters.

Job 38:30. The waters are hid as *with* a stone, and the face of the deep is *frozen*.

Genesis 1:3. And God said, Let there be light: and there was light.

Genesis 1:9-10. And God said, Let the waters under the heaven be gathered together unto one place, and let the dry *land* appear:[......] and

God called the dry *land* Earth.

Over a six day period God restored the heavens and the earth *which are now*. He renewed the face of the earth, and created a new order of carbon-based life-forms, including modern-day man created in His own image and likeness.

Psalms 104:30. Thou sendest forth thy spirit, they are created: and thou renewest the face of the earth.

In other words, the heavens and earth which now exist are a restored generation of the heavens and earth of old, which were created by God "in the beginning" as per Genesis 1:1.

Since the foundation of the world (the 6 day restoration of the heavens and the earth and the creation of Adam), modern-day man created in the image and likeness of God has *inherited* the petrified remains of the silicon-based biological life forms from the previous world, now transitioned to stone.

But by and large, they have been mistakenly identified as being massive ancient geological structures. This includes the many tabletop mountains, or mesas, found across the earth, which before being hewn down in the previous world, were gigantic, silicon-based, towering trees of an almost unbelievable height. All that remained were their enormous stumps and root systems, which were left in the ground. *(Daniel 4:26.)*

The petrified remains of prehistoric creatures and trees, the size of which goes literally off the charts, have been *inherited* by the inhabitants of *this* world, from the aeon or "the world that then was" back in the heavens of old *(2 Peter 3:6)* and misidentified as being ancient geological structures.

In other words, the generation of the heavens and the earth, *which are now,* bear witness to the aeon or world, which existed, and perished, back in the heavens and the earth *of old*, which God had created *in the beginning*.

Hence, when God restored Light to the pitch-black heavens, and renewed the face of the barren and lifeless earth, a record of death and destruction of life on a massive scale, already existed beneath Adam's feet, in the form of the geological and fossil record. An *inheritance* if you like, from the primordial world.

Death entered this present aeon or world, from the moment Adam disobeyed God and fell into sin. Hence death (the wages of sin) was

Inheritance

.... rited by all of mankind.

The Bible as a whole, but especially the Book of Genesis, portrays the Earth and its waters as being a circular, fixed, and stationary realm, separated from the waters above the heavens by a firmament (or vault) which contains the celestial bodies.

Prior to the flood of Noah, the circle of the flat earth, had 4 major rivers, no individual continents or oceans, and was completely surrounded by the waters of the deep. Hence, for about 1,650 years, mankind had virtually unhindered access to every quarter of the entire habitable realm of Earth. Every equal-arm cross in existence today, from the swastika to the crucifix, was originally based upon the circle of the earth with its 4 major rivers.

At some point in time after the creation of Adam and Eve, and as the population numbers grew, the sons of God (extraterrestrial angelic beings) were attracted by the beauty of the daughters of men. The surrounding context suggests that the sons of God forcibly took of whosoever they chose for a wife. If so, then without human consent, the sons of God sired children with these daughter of men, whose offspring were known as the giants, the mighty men, the men of renown.*(Genesis 6.)*

Although not actually recorded, it's very likely there existed at the time, a worldwide trade network, organized by the 'mighty men', for the distribution of the highly addictive chemical compound, 'Adrenochrome'. Just as today in the post-flood world, this would have been obtained by harvesting Adrenochrome from the blood of the hunted down, abducted, and highly traumatized children of men.

Genesis 6:5. God saw that the wickedness of man was great in the earth, and that every imagination of the thoughts of his heart was only evil continually.

It is also highly likely that drinking the blood of terrorized children, was one of the primary reasons for the impending flood. For almost immediately after the flood, God prohibited the consumption of blood, human or otherwise. *(Genesis 9:4).*

Everyone was warned of what was coming, but only Noah listened to God, and the rest is a watery history.

After 40 days and 40 nights of torrential rain, the entire earth, including its mountains were completely submerged, primarily by fresh water. As the floodwaters subsided and drained from the surface of the earth, they froze to form a boundary, a barrier of ice completely surrounding the flat, circular earth. This is why the Ice Wall known today as Antarctica, accounts for 90 percent of Earth's total ice volume and 70 percent of its fresh water. It is the boundary set in place by God, to restrain the waters from covering the earth again.

Psalms 104:9. Thou hast set a bound that they [THE WATERS] may not pass over; that they turn not again to cover the earth.

The wicked practise of harvesting Adrenochrome from the blood of abducted and highly traumatized innocent children, which so many of the world's elite are addicted to today, started again *after* the flood, most likely with Nimrod, who was "a mighty hunter" before the LORD. *(Genesis 10:9.)*

For there is nothing good whatsoever, in the term "a mighty hunter," rather, it's used in a derogatory sense. Likewise, Esau we're told was a "cunning hunter'.' *(Genesis 25:27).* Yet again a derogatory term.

Many times throughout the Old Testament, young children were tortured and terrorized as they were "passed through the fire to Molech." *(2 Kings 23:10.)* A most heinous practise indeed, forbidden and despised by God, and which was the primary reason for the 70 year exile of the Israelites in Babylon.

Stone Monuments

Every nation on earth has descended from Adam and Eve (the mother of all living) via one of the 3 sons of Noah, and their wives. Noah had first hand experience of life during the time of Genesis 6. An experience which I'm sure was passed down the generations by word of mouth.

Although considered myth by many, multiple cultures across the earth have retained a 'collective memory' of a worldwide flood, which only a few survived. Likewise tales of demi-gods and giants are abundant in folklore worldwide. Many of whom had a passion for human blood, as in Jack the giant Slayer's;

"Fe, *Fi, Fo, Fum.* I *smell* the *blood* of an *Englishman*".

In the semi-mythical story of the founding of Britain, Albion (a contemporary of Heracles) was the primeval man, a giant son of Poseidon, the Greek god of the sea. Albion founded a country inhabited by his giant descendants until about 1100 years before Julius Caesar's invasion of Britain.

It was almost certainly these pre-flood giants, the men of renown, who built the megalithic stone structures that can be found all over the Earth. The weight of some of these blocks which are precision cut and fit perfectly together, is incredible. The largest stone at Avebury Circle, England for example, weighs over 40 tons.

How can we be certain it was the giants who originally cut these stones and erected the Monoliths?

Well, after the flood of Noah which wiped out the giants, and as the world began to repopulate, mankind now lacked the ability to cut and perfectly fit together massive blocks of stone. Instead, when constructing the tower at Babel, they now had to improvise by baking bricks rather than use cut stone, and mix a primitive mortar to use as a binding agent.

Genesis 11:3. And they said one to another, Go to, let us make brick, and burn them throughly. And they had brick *for stone*, and slime had they for *morter*.

Again, it's almost certain that the Great Pyramid and the Sphinx were constructed during the pre-flood age of the giants, and were merely **inherited** by the Egyptians approximately 900 years or so after the flood.

Likewise, Stonehenge in England, was **inherited** by the Druids who are known to have made additions to the original site, and the megalithic stone structures in South America were **inherited** by the Incas and the Mayans etc. When the Incas and Aztecs arrived, they discovered cities, pyramids and temples, such as Ollantaytambo in Peru, which were already erected, and they just moved in.

This of course, wouldn't sit too well with the official mainstream narrative. Instead history has to be fabricated, if for no other reason, than to leave out the age of the giants, who God destroyed by a flood as recorded in Genesis 6.

They would rather have us believe that the estimated 2,300,000 limestone and granite blocks that make up the Great Pyramid were pushed, pulled, shoved and dragged into place using multiple ropes hauled by alternating teams of thousands of 6 foot tall, muscular slaves or conscript labourers. Seriously?

The average weight of the blocks is 2.5 imperial tons and the granite blocks within the Kings Chamber weighing up to 88 tons. Having been quarried with copper chisels and wooden mallets at Aswan, these massive granite blocks were then ferried down the River Nile, a distance today, of 543 miles.

I couldn't help but to chuckle to myself when I heard one presenter remark how a 2 ton block was positioned every 20 minutes, day and night, for 20 years! Do you see the absurdity and the impossibility of the official narrative, when you pause for a while, and think about things logically? The truth is far more likely to be, that as the world began to repopulate after the flood, and after the confusion of tongues at Babel, certain groups and families migrated to the land, since known as Egypt.

Upon arrival, they discovered the Sphinx and the Great Pyramid, partially, or completely buried beneath the vast residue of silt and mud left behind after the flood of Noah. Not only did they *inherit* the Great Pyramid, they *inherited* it without a clue of what its original purpose was, nor who had actually built it in the first place.

No doubt, future generations would gaze in awe at these giant stone monuments, and maybe even stop to wonder who had actually built them? I'd love to know what the official narrative was at the time; the cover story used by the authorities to justify the existence of these impossible structures. Either way, I think it highly likely that when pondering these incredible monuments, the local residents at the time would say;

"They just don't build them like this any more, do they?"

The original builders also had a truly remarkable understanding of trigonometry and astronomy. Traditional historians can only speculate how the interior of the Great Pyramid with its regal chambers, grand gallery and ascending and descending passages were constructed. And how the 3 pyramids at the Giza Plateau are so perfectly aligned, not only with the 4 cardinal points of this earthly realm, but also with Polaris and the Orion's Belt in the heavenly realm high above.

They were also aware it seems, that due to the solid limestone plateau it was built on, the Great Pyramid had no need for special foundations. How would the builders have known this?

Hidden History

It has been said that;

> No branch of world history has been suppressed as energetically or effectively as the history of the Americas before the nineteenth-century. In fact, the familiar story of Columbus and his dealings with Ferdinand and Isabella, the "Catholic Monarchs," which is the supposed cornerstone of American history, is mostly a product of the early nineteenth-century. In vain will you search for records bearing on such events or personalities before that time.

On January 6, 1858, 'The Raftsman Journal' published an intriguing article called 'Antiquities in America', discussing "many of the ruins and structures around this continent that have not been discussed by official history".

The article reads in part;

> How few reflect on the fact that America is an old dominion – the seat of an ancient, mighty empire. These facts are opening themselves every day to the eyes of the astonished world, and it is to be hoped that the spirit of inquiry, which seems at present to animate all classes of learned men, may throw light on the early history of this remarkable region.

America was once the seat of an ancient, mighty empire? What on earth is that supposed to mean? If it were true, then surely we would have been taught about this "mighty empire" long ago. Wouldn't we? John Bach McMaster's 'A Brief History of the United States' was originally published in 1871. In the Preface it reads;

> Before the task (of preparing this book) was undertaken, it was known that there was misapprehension or misrepresentation in regard to the earlier periods, and that details were often discolored or disguised by political, sectional, or local prejudices. Many grave questions, too, are still in dispute without the possibility of reaching secure conclusions.

We are left to wonder on the nature of the grave questions "still in dispute" and how they might relate to the "misrepresentation of earlier periods". Neither are we told which particular details were disguised for political reasons etc. The historical record of a bygone age maybe? One which by and large has been covered up, skewed or redesignated to fit with a fabricated mainstream narrative?

On the face of it, any theory which suggests that an entire period of history has been covered up or disguised for political reasons etc. effectively erases millions of people who lived in the area during that period. Indeed, perhaps this has been the case.

Hypothetically speaking then, if indeed an entire block or era of history has been hidden from the public record, we are left to wonder what justification the controllers thought they might have for doing so? For the benefit of the public at large? I very much doubt it. I think it far more likely to be for reasons of power and financial gain of exceeding wealth.

Or possibly their motive was born out of fear?

The New World

The *"New World"* (as opposed to the old world) is a term used specifically for the Americas. The term gained prominence in the early 16th century.

The arrival of the Spanish Conquistadors in Yucatán in the 1520's, signalled the beginning of the end for Mayan civilisation. Under the banner of the Cross (Papal Catholicism) it is estimated that during the initial Spanish conquest of the Americas, up to eight million indigenous people died, primarily through the spread of diseases.

Simultaneously, the eighteenth and nineteenth century wars and atrocities waged by the Europeans against Native Americans also resulted in hundreds of thousands, or more likely, millions of deaths.

The mistreatment, enslavement and killing of Native Americans continued for centuries, in every area of the Americas, including the areas that would become Canada, the United States, Mexico, Brazil, and countries such as Paraguay, Chile, and Argentina.

Could the true reason for this deliberate, prolonged and barbaric act of mass genocide that lasted for centuries, have been to eradicate the last generation of humanity in the Americas, who still retained a collective memory of a cataclysmic event, that brought about an abrupt change in social conditions, and even to history itself?

A Great Reset of sorts, in the historical timeline, but one not recorded as such, in the mainstream narrative?

Since the early 1900's, there has been a major cover-up, especially by organizations such as the Smithsonian Institution, to make us believe that America was first colonized by Asian peoples migrating through the Bering Strait around 15,000 years ago.

From a Biblical perspective of course, there were no Asian people, nor any other race of modern-day man (created in the image of God) on Earth 15,000 years ago. The controllers had to introduce such a concept, in an attempt to give credence to the theory of Evolution and the theoretical Big Bang.

There are however, thousands of burial mounds all over America which the Natives claim were there a long time before them. Many of these burial mounds show traces of a developed civilization, and giant human skeletal remains have frequently been found, that have not been reported in the media and news outlets.

As I understand, when these giant skeletons have been discovered, they have promptly been confiscated by the authorities, and placed under lock and key by the Smithsonian Institution.

These burial mounds and skeletal remains have their origins in the antediluvian age, and just like the ancient stone monuments, have been *inherited* by the inhabitants of the post-flood world.

Some might say, "hmm", that's quite fascinating and maybe it's true. Some relics from the ancient past could well have been inherited by a later civilization or society. But how is that relevant for us today?

Maybe it's time to take a closer look at certain aspects of the official record, and see what is hidden in plain sight, then to reconsider and re-educate ourselves. For we tend not to see the vast amount of evidence "hidden in plain sight", in the environment around us. *Not* because it is *not* there, *but* because we tend to overlook any evidence that is *not* supposed to be there.

That evidence is visible in the infrastructure and architecture across the entire realm we call Earth. We have been indoctrinated to believe that those who created this glorious architecture, done so during the days of the horse and cart, a period that official history refers to as the Middle Ages aka the Dark Age.

Time and again when comparing the visual evidence around us with the official narrative, we find glaring inconsistencies and at times, even impossibilities which just don't add up. For the controllers of history seem to have compressed the construction of the visual evidence into a timeline which has been shortened or manipulated.

For several years I've spent a lot of time as an amateur researcher of history and learned to my dismay that the official narrative of many historical events relies heavily on guesswork and is usually a little suspect, to say the very least. Or as Napoleon so succinctly put it;

"History is a set of lies that certain people have agreed upon."

It's reached a point in fact, where over the last year or so, I've experienced a major shift in my understanding of history. History has been grossly misrepresented, and in some cases never happened at all. At least, not in the manner we are told. From time to time certain individuals suddenly appear on the scene, and much like phantoms, haunt the pages of history for a while. It would seem that the controllers have used such individuals to disguise and discredit much of the evidence for the old world.

It's fairly widely accepted now, that much of world history has been hidden, falsified, or at the very best sanitized, to fit an official narrative, especially over the last 400 years or so.

Some folk have long had the sense that things have never been quite what they seem, or what they were taught, whilst others appear to have minds that are closed off completely to anything outside of the controlled narrative.

To the latter, I would ask; is there anyone who has not gazed in awe at the intricate detail of the sculpted masonry, and the beautiful architecture of our old churches, cathedrals, palaces, town halls and government buildings?

Have you never paused for a moment to wonder who built them? And why such marvels are never built in similar style today? Like the early Egyptians who gazed in awe at the Great Pyramid, have you not gazed in awe at a Grand Cathedral and said;

"They just don't build them like this any more, do they?"

For I certainly have. In fact, for most of my life, I've been amazed by the resplendent architecture of the grand old buildings we see in our towns and cities, but have always believed the narrative, that most were built within the last 300 years or so. Nevertheless, I always remained puzzled as to how they managed to achieve such marvels back in the olden days of the horse and cart.

Don't get me wrong, I have no doubt in man's ability to design and build incredible structures, but certainly not of the magnificent style I'm referring to, and not during the time period we are told.

Revised Timeline?

The concept of a revised timeline or a "new chronology" is most fully explained by Anatoly Fomenko in his 2002 book; *History: Fiction or Science?* originally published in Russian.

Labelled a crazy, pseudo-historical, conspiracy theorist by many, Fomenko argues that the events of antiquity generally attributed to the civilizations of the Roman empire, ancient Greece and ancient Egypt, actually occurred during the Middle Ages, more than a thousand years later. Some even propose that the Roman empire fell suddenly, rather than a gradual fall.

Fomenko proposes that, the written history of humankind goes only as far back as 800 AD, how there is almost no information about events between 800 AD and 1000 AD, and most known historical events actually took place from 1000 AD to 1500 AD.

He also presents a reasonable argument, that world history prior to 1600 AD has been widely falsified to suit the interests of a number of different conspirators including the Vatican, the Holy Roman Empire, and the Russian House of Romanov, all working together to obscure the "true" history of the world, and centred around a global empire called the "Russian Horde".

Although I wouldn't necessarily agree with all he proposes, such as the "Russian Horde", I do feel that Fomenko is on the right track. We have been indoctrinated to accept a timeline which has been falsified to suit an agenda, and to the extent where a possible eight hundred years or more of earlier history has been folded into a more recent timeline.

Consider for a moment, the numerous grand Cathedrals around the world.

It's true that prior to the Industrial Revolution, the cost of manual labour was relatively low compared with the high cost of wages today. But this needs to be balanced with the time element involved and the production costs, where automated, mass produced concrete, steel and glass etc. are relatively cheap. Not to mention the absolute nightmare of the logistics involved back in the Middle Ages.

Raw materials first had to be mined or quarried, transported by horse and cart to be refined and processed, then manually loaded onto wagons once again, before being harnessed to mules or oxen, and transported to the build site. In some cases 100 miles or more.

Never mind the amount of engineering disciplines required to excavate the footings, install the drain work, to erect the scaffolding, and the huge number of skilled and unskilled labour required.

They achieved all of this with primitive roads by today's standards, without electricity, power tools, diamond cut blades, and no modern-day heavy machinery and lifting equipment.

Wouldn't it be a far easier task in this modern-day age of hi-tech machinery, power tools, delivery lorries and tower cranes that can reach over 200 feet and lift 18 metric tons?

And yet it rarely happens, if it actually happens at all.

The list of reasons why these majestic constructions were as good as impossible to erect during the time frame we're told, makes it quite easy to realize there is something very awry with the given timeline. Who built them? When did it all stop? And why?

Such questions are also as good as impossible to find official answers for, and trying to do so, becomes much like playing a game of Charades in the dark. For there is no photographic evidence for anything prior to the nineteenth century, and of course, nobody can travel back in time, to see for themselves what was really going on.

When I first stumbled across this strange enigma, I remember thinking, "This is ridiculous". How is it even possible, for an entire period of history to have been hidden from us? And even if it were true, which I'm sure it's not, then what exactly has been hidden?

And why would "the controllers" consider it to be of such vital importance, and to their advantage to conceal whatever it is they are hiding, from the general public in the first place?

Why invest so much time, money and effort into doing so? Are they afraid of something? If so, then what are they afraid of? And why?

Well, it seems quite possible that something major, and of a world changing nature occurred, probably during the period from 1650 to 1815, which culminated in 1816; known as;

'The Year Without a Summer'.

The Art of Repurpose

"When plunder becomes a way of life for a group of men in a society, over the course of time they create for themselves a legal system that authorizes it and a moral code that glorifies it." – *Frédéric Bastiat, Economic Sophisms, 1848.*

Constructed we're told as fortified settlements in the 16th and the 17th centuries, thousands of magnificent "star cities", star forts" or "star stations" are scattered all over Europe, the UK, America and most other parts of the world. The 16th century 'Fort St. Elmo' in Malta is one of the oldest and most iconic star forts, spanning about 50,400 square metres. Sounds pretty impressive wouldn't you say? Yet when carefully studying city layouts like Amsterdam, Paris and Copenhagen, it becomes increasingly clear that each entire city was in fact, originally designed as a star city. Geneva for example.

Many have only been discovered in more recent times due to the availability of aerial and satellite images of the earth's surface. And Google Earth of course. For consisting of perfectly aligned streets, bastions, lakes, complex canal systems, waterways and islands, their precise geometrical layout can only be fully appreciated when viewed from above.

How such precision was achieved 400 to 500 years ago as we are told, beggars belief, for even today with modern technology and overhead drones, I very much doubt such cities and landscapes could be replicated with quite the same degree of accuracy. In every instance the intricate network of star city waterways eventually flow into rivers, which flow into the oceans which are all interconnected worldwide.

Furthermore when studying the photos of these truly remarkable star cities which can be found on the Internet, the official line that they were constructed for fortification and defence purposes just doesn't quite ring true somehow. In fact, star cities raise far more questions than there are official answers to. Not in the least because they are virtually ignored by mainstream academia.

It now seems apparent that the nineteenth century drawings, plans and descriptions of these truly remarkable structures have been manipulated, and hence should be considered as fraudulent. This is why some claim these remarkable and precise geometric wonders, couldn't possibly have been constructed by man.

The true builders they say, were visitors to earth of extraterrestrial origin. Others maintain they were designed by time travellers from the future.

We'll return to these magnificent star cities later, and what may have been their true purpose. And how their construction dates further back than the time period we've been told. Fobbed off as being built for defence, these star stations once served a far nobler purpose.

In the meanwhile, please bear in mind that the controllers of the narrative (known or unknown) and those who manipulate the public, will go to extreme lengths to cover up their nefarious agenda. Although they have no empathy whatsoever for the general public, they live in fear of being exposed for who they are, and for all to see. People have been deliberately dumbed down, but they are not brain-dead, which is why, perhaps more than ever before, folk are slowly beginning to "wake up." For if the last couple of years have taught us anything, it is the extent to which our tyrannical governments and complicit mainstream media will go, not only to deceive us into believing a rampant killer virus was on the loose, but also to keep us in the dark.

Wrote George Orwell in his dystopian novel, 1984;

> Every record has been destroyed or falsified, every book rewritten, every picture has been repainted, every statue and street building has been renamed, every date has been altered. And the process is continuing day by day and minute by minute. History has stopped. Nothing exists except an endless present in which the Party is always right.

Photography

The first permanent photograph of a camera image was made in 1825 by Joseph Nicéphore Niépce using a sliding wooden box camera made by Charles and Vincent Chevalier in Paris.

The use of photographic film was pioneered by George Eastman, whose first camera, which he called the "Kodak", was first offered for sale in 1888. These early cameras were difficult to set up and took time to set up for a single photo.

Every depiction of every building etc. prior to 1830 or thereabouts, thus relied solely upon diagrams, sketches and artist's impressions. As good as they may be, any of these are open to manipulation.

I can recall how back in the late 1950's, my Aunty Kath was the first member of our family to purchase a hand-held camera, the 'Kodak Brownie'. I also remember having to wait 2 to 3 weeks for the film to be developed, before we could see the photographs. I was wearing a pair of short trousers and a sailor's hat, courtesy of Uncle Ed, which he'd kept from his Royal Navy days. The hat that is, not the short trousers.

Aunty Kath was also the first in the family to buy a new car, a white Mini. I can even remember the numberplate; SNJ 927. She could even start the engine by using an ignition key, unlike Uncle Ed, who had to make do with a manual crank handle to fire up his old Ford Prefect. I remember his car quite well, but have totally forgotten the number plate.

Everything was completely different back in the 50's, 60's and 70's of course. Even the summer sky, which was blue, crisp and clear, with sharply defined clouds, and with a different sun intensity. For those were the days when thousands upon thousands of swallows migrated to the UK each summer, to build their nests of mud under the eaves of our houses, and perch lined up on the telegraph cables for as far as the eye could see. But not any more. The change started in the mid to late 80's, as I recall, and continues to this day.

The change in the narrative however, began long before I was born. For I believe the change can be traced back to the early nineteenth century, and was kickstarted with London's 'Great Exhibition of the Works of Industry of All Nations' which was held in 1851.

In 1768 'The Encyclopedia Britannica' began publication, and people began to have access to quality information. In 1875, John D. Rockefeller, bought the venerable reference source, and failed to let anyone know of the changes being made by the new editors at the Cambridge University Press. In 1903, Rockefeller founded 'The

General Education Board' for a cost of $129 million.

The very fact that John D. Rockefeller, who is considered to be the wealthiest American of all time, was instrumental in making such a radical change to both the field of information and the education system, should set alarm bells ringing.

The Nobel Peace Prize was awarded to American physicist Arthur Holly Compton for free energy extraction called zero point energy in 1923, yet not one college textbook will let you know that, because another tactic adopted by the Rockefeller's was to select only approved authors for school textbooks. Rockefeller money has effectively controlled the education system since 1920.

The controllers didn't rewrite history from scratch, but rewrote the historical narrative to fit their own agenda. Starting from a very young age, we have unwittingly been required to learn their fabricated version of history, via the compulsory education system.

In fact it reaches the point where it is impossible to say for sure, what happened, when it happened, and in some cases, even if it happened at all. There is a secretive parallel world the 'controllers' of history would prefer you not know.

Times of Change

According to Statista, the current number of *smartphone* users in the *world* today is 6.378 billion, and this means 80.63% of the world's population can take an instant photograph at any given moment, at any given location. The point being, we live in an entirely different world to the world experienced by our ancestors of just 130 years ago. That's not to mention the instant modern-day communication network, and instant access to the world of information.

Direct handwritten weekly news sheets circulated widely in Venice as early as 1566, but the first printed, weekly newspapers weren't published until 1609. Typically, they were heavily censored by the government (no surprise there of course) and reported only foreign news and current prices. The first regular daily newspaper to be printed in England, the 'Daily Courant', was launched in 1702.

Hypothetically speaking then, if a major and world-changing event had taken place during a period which ended say, 5 or 6 generations ago, and the "controllers" modified or deleted the historical record, would we be any the wiser for it today?

What if any physical evidence for this hypothetical major event of say 400 years ago, were to be hidden, or redesignated to fit a contrived timeline and a rewritten 'official' narrative? How would we know either way? We're talking of a time remember, prior to the invention of the camera, and without an instant communication and information network.

I suspect most would automatically believe what they read or what they've been told, until something crops up to upset the status quo, so to speak. And then what? Reject anything that contradicts the official line? Or take a big risk and challenge the status quo?

During the exploration of Cuzco, Peru, in 1533, Conquistador Francisco Pizarro was so impressed with what he'd discovered, that he wrote back to King Charles I of Spain, saying:

"This city is the greatest and the finest ever seen in this country or anywhere in the Indies... We can assure your Majesty that it is so beautiful and has such fine buildings that it would be remarkable even in Spain." [Credit:Wikipedia]

Evidently, architectural structures of grandeur and finery that rivalled, if not surpassed those in Europe, could be found in South America in the mid Sixteenth Century. Who built them?

According to the official controlled narrative, it was the hundreds of thousands of early Spanish settlers,who arrived there during the Peruvian colonial era. This would be long after Francisco Pizarro had already reported the existence of all this splendid architecture. Lima for example. Do you not find that somewhat bewildering?

Could the same be true of North America and Canada? For if so, the existence of Greco-Roman architecture would be nigh impossible to explain, because in contrast to Europe, America and Canada do not have an official Greco-Roman history.

Hypothetically, if such style of unexplainable architecture were to be found in America, could it be possible that in time, these buildings were revealed to the public, under the pretext of having been recently constructed, but only on a ***temporary*** basis, for the mysterious World Expositions? Having served their purpose, what if these alleged ***temporary*** structures were deliberately destroyed?

In 1923, pioneer film-maker and Freemason, Cecil. B. DeMille built the largest set in movie history for his silent, early Technicolour epic, 'The Ten Commandments'. Constructed way out in the desert near Guadalupe, California, 'The City of the Pharaoh' consisted of a

750 feet long city wall with a 109 feet tall entrance gate embossed with horses and chariots, a massive Egyptian temple, twelve 5-ton sphinxes, eight huge lions, and four 40-ton statues of Ramses II.

When filming was completed, DeMille ordered that the entire edifice be razed to the ground, and secretly buried beneath the shifting sand dunes. And there it lay, entombed and forgotten for the next 60 years.

In 1983, and inspired by a strange rumour he'd overheard in a bar, an enterprising young film maker named Peter Brosnan embarked upon a 30 year mission to locate and excavate the lost city.

Brosnan recorded his 30 year battle with red tape and the authorities to achieve his goal in his 2017 documentary, The *Lost City of Cecil B. DeMille.*

Well, that's the official story anyway, for there are those who maintain the city of Pharaoh already existed as part of America's hidden history. It was merely unearthed and renovated by Cecil B. DeMille, who was previously aware of its existence. Once it had served its purpose, he ordered the entire construction site to be destroyed, buried and hence remain hidden again.

Whether true or not I wouldn't know, and I'm not suggesting the ancient Egyptians travelled to America, but Columbus certainly wasn't the first to arrive at her shores. The Vikings led by Leif Erickson reached North America around 1000 A.D. almost 500 years before Columbus. But even the Vikings were probably not the first expedition to do so.

Interestingly, most historians regarded the Viking sagas as fictional, until unmistakable Norse artefacts and archaeological finds were discovered in Newfoundland, Canada around 1960, completely shattered their world view.

According to the Owlcation website;

There is no specific mention of any Egyptian expedition to the

New World, but there are some tantalizing clues that they may have reached it. The most telling clue that the Egyptians may have reached North America comes in the form of the Cocaine Mummies.

In 1992, a young German toxicologist Dr. Svetlana Balabanova, was examining a collection of mummies at the German State Museum of Egyptian Art, when she discovered traces of cocaine and nicotine in the hair of Henut Taui, an Ancient Egyptian priestess whose remains were mummified, circa 1000 B.C.

She immediately realized how severe the implications of her findings were, so she tested, and re-tested, and tested her results again to be certain that there was no mistake. There wasn't, and furthermore, she found traces of the same drugs in some of the other ancient Egyptian corpses.

But when Balabanova went public with her findings, she was met with hostility and contempt from her colleagues and the historical community at large. They were afraid to face up to the possibility that their understanding of ancient history might need to be re-examined and rewritten.

For these narcotics were not to be found anywhere on the African continent *until after* Columbus voyaged the seas, a fact which left archaeologists and historians scratching their heads, trying to figure out how this might have occurred. For Cocaine is made exclusively from the coca plant, which does not grow outside of South America.

Yet chemical analysis of the ingredients used to embalm these Egyptian mummies shows the unmistakable and unexplainable presence of "cocaine." *(Credit: Owlcation.)*

As far as I know, the jury is still out on this one. For we have a tendency to look back on our own history with a preconceived notion, that previous peoples were less intelligent and certainly less innovative than ourselves.

Thousands of antediluvian structures were once preserved beneath the mammoth residue of mud and silt which would have been leftover by the great deluge in Noah's day. Many of which have now been excavated, especially over the centuries since the destruction of Jerusalem in 70A.D.

The legendary lost city of Atlantis apart, numerous underwater cities and monuments have been discovered around the world. But these date no further back than the time of the giants, the mighty men, the men of renown, who God destroyed during Noah's Flood.

Discovered in 1987 on the seabed, a few miles off the coast of Japan, the Yonaguni Monument, is a massive 164 feet long by 65 feet wide rectangular, stacked pyramid-like structure. Known as the Pyramid City, the oldest pyramids found on Earth, are located on the seabed, just off the coast of Crimea. The point being, these underwater ruins have been *inherited* from the antediluvian world.

Yet there is no comparison whatsoever between the comparatively crude, megalithic stone monuments erected in the pre-flood world, and the majestic architecture of the monumental brick, marble, concrete and stone buildings constructed over the course of the present post-flood world.

The difference however between the antediluvian Pyramid and the post-flood Cathedral, for example, is of itself, a *monumental* one. The question is; who built them?

The basic principles of these magnificent buildings is always the same and their architectural qualities remain unrivalled. Would it be unreasonable to suggest that this fact alone, indicates the existence of a former advanced civilization, no longer with us today?

Parliament Buildings

Consider for example, the mind blowing architecture of the British Columbia Parliament Building, which we are told was built on Vancouver Island in the late 1800's.

Wikipedia informs us that from 1860 to 1898 the Legislature of the Colony of Vancouver Island was housed in the first permanent building on the island, a simple two-storey wooden structure. This, along with four smaller wooden buildings, were known colloquially as "the Birdcages". But they were cold and draughty, and the water leaked in through the roof when it rained.

Rather than replace the five wooden structures with moderate sized masonry buildings, the council decided to go the whole hog, and take the new building to an entirely different level.

So the powers that be got their heads together, and hatched a plan to hold an architectural competition. The entrant who came up with the most elaborate design, would be awarded the honour of constructing the brand new legislative building.

The competition was finally won by architect, Francis Rattenbury, a

25 year old immigrant from England, and a bit of a scoundrel from all accounts. However, it was agreed that the new British Columbia Parliament Buildings, would be designed in the Neo-Baroque, Renaissance Revival style.

Construction work on the new parliament building started in 1893 and was completed in 1897. This towering architectural wonder topped with ten blue domes, could well be the most beautiful Parliament Building in the world.

With a 500-feet long facade and two huge pavilions either end, the resplendent architecture of the beautifully sculpted stonework, and the perfectly designed, central, domed rotunda are absolutely breath taking. And this majestic structure was built on a remote island when the population was just a few hundred people?

Consider the logistics involved. Where did the hundreds of thousands of tons of building material come from? The concrete, the brick, the stone, the wood, the metal and the multiple tons of marble used to furnish the interior?

And that's without taking into account preparing all the groundwork, the drainage, excavating the footings, building the foundations and the huge amount of scaffolding required.

Yet we are told this majestic structure was completed on an island in a mere four years. Forgive my sarcasm, but, Yeah; right! The magnitude of deceit is overwhelming.

This masterpiece of noble architecture is more likely to be an old world structure, discovered and *inherited* by the new arrivals to the shores of Canada, and its existence was attributed to a 25 year old, Irish immigrant.

We have been hoodwinked into believing a false narrative. For the British Columbia Parliament Building is in all likelihood, much older than the wooden shacks known as the Birdcages, it allegedly replaced.

Can this be proven? Where is the evidence? you ask.

The Empirical evidence is right in front of our eyes, and always has been. But we need to wake up, and use our God-given senses and logic to see it.

Westminster

Then we have the magnificent Palace of Westminster, which stands glorious on an 8 acre site, on the Thames Embankment in London, now the seat of the UK Parliament. We are told the original building was gutted by fire and virtually demolished in 1834.

Like their Canadian counterparts, the British parliament also decided to go the whole hog, and take the new building to another level. They too held a competition.

According the the UK Parliament;

> In 1836, the commissioners organised a public competition to design a new Palace in either of these styles. They received 97 entries, each identifiable only by a pseudonym or symbol. From these, the commissioners chose four, of which they were unanimous in preferring entry number 64 which bore the emblem of the Portcullis. This was the entry submitted by Charles Barry, who had proposed a Gothic-styled palace in harmony with the surviving buildings.

The building contains over 1,100 rooms organised symmetrically around two series of courtyards, and which has a floor area of 1,210,680 square feet. And then we have the iconic Big Ben, the heaviest of the five bells housed in the Elizabeth Tower.

This majestic structure as it stands today, was rebuilt so we're told, from 1840-1876, when the site;

"was extended into the river Thames by reclaiming land, to a total of about eight acres." *(Credit; UK Parliament).*

Exactly how this was achieved we're not told, but it must have been an extremely unpleasant task. The exceptionally hot summer of 1858 was known as the "Great Stink", due to the smell of untreated human waste and industrial effluent that was present on the banks of the River Thames.

The truth is more likely to be, that the palace with its elegant spires, towers and domes, is an old world building, ***inherited*** and ***repurposed*** by the British Government during the mid nineteenth century. It is highly dubious that this massive building was constructed in the manner we're told on land reclaimed from the river Thames.

A postcard photograph of Westminster Bridge and the Houses of Parliament circa 1910, with pedestrians, horse-drawn hansom cabs, an early motorized vehicle and trams in the foreground tells it all. A brief moment captured in time, of a society in the transition stage from natural horse power to engineered horse power.

I cannot discredit the skill and ability of those in the nineteenth century, but find it hard to believe this majestic building was constructed by a generation who existed a mere 50 or 60 years before the photograph was taken.

Can such a claim be proven? Obviously not. But it's much like me saying that one hundred years ago, my grandfather worked in the mobile phone industry. A far cry from his actual work as a stoker for the Merchant Navy. Shovelling tons of coal into a ship's furnace for eight hours a day, was a career certainly not to be envied.

I trust that the point I'm trying to raise here is making some sort of sense. For many such photographs taken in the late nineteenth and early twentieth century have a similar tale to tell.

A people without the tools and the technological ability to construct the glorious architecture surrounding them. Yet we are expected to believe that their recent forebears of just a few decades previous, had the remarkable ability to achieve all of this?

The 19th and early 20th century was a time of transition from the old world into the modern era. Not only was the old technology being phased out, but the old world infrastructure was being destroyed or repurposed.

There are numerous reasons to question the official historical narrative. If you, the reader, have remained with me thus far, my hope is that you will continue, and reach a similar conclusion.

Although there are many unanswered questions, you will inevitably start to see things in a different light when pondering all of these structures, and the time period they were supposedly built in.

Welcome to the Alternative History Community. It is growing rapidly. For those whose interest is peaked, and who wish to re-educate themselves, I highly recommend Ewaranon's eye-opening, 6-hour long Documentary on 'YouTube' titled;

"The Lost History Of The Flat Earth".

Perception

As noted by researcher, Michelle Gibson, in the nineteenth century, following the American Civil War, stories and inexpensive Dime Novels depicting the American West and frontier life were becoming very popular.

In 1883, Buffalo Bill's Wild West was founded in North Platte, Nebraska, when the former U.S. Army scout and bison hunter, William F (Buffalo Bill) Cody turned his real life adventure into the first outdoor western show.

All sorts of characters from the frontier were incorporated into the show's program. Shooting exhibitions were also in the line-up, with extensive shooting displays and many a trick shot.

Rodeo events, involving rough and dangerous activities performed by Cowboys with Horses, Buffalo, Moose, Elk and even Bears, also featured, along with theatrical re-enactments of battle scenes, characteristic western scenes, and even hunts.

While some of the storylines and characters were based on true events, others were fictional or sensationalized. None more so than the American Indians. Hundreds of thousand were subject to years of genocide and slavery, and by the 1880's, most American Indians had been confined to reservations, often in areas of the West that appeared least desirable to white settlers.

Buffalo Bill's 'Wild West' toured Europe eight times, the first four tours between 1887 and 1892, and the last four from 1902 to 1906. Performing in France, Austria, Germany, Belgium, Italy, Poland, Hungary, Romania and the Ukraine, Buffalo Bill and his Wild West show had influenced the public's perception of America, across an entire continent. *(Credit:Wikipedia.)*

The first tour was in 1887 as part of the American Exhibition, which coincided with the Golden Jubilee of Queen Victoria. After its extraordinary sell-out success in London, the tour made stops in Birmingham and Manchester before returning to the United States in May, 1888, for a short summer tour.

A return tour was made in 1891-92, including Cardiff, Wales, and Glasgow, Scotland, in the itinerary.

Do you think the controllers of history managed to get the message across?

The cowboy became the symbol for the West of the late 19th century, often depicted in popular culture as a glamorous or heroic figure.

I think it fair to say that the majority of folk like myself, who were born in the mid-twentieth century, were subtly conditioned from the start, to accept a controlled historical narrative of the American Wild West.

A perceived new world, empty of infrastructure, apart from a plethora of wigwams and pine cabins, with plenty of land and gold for the taking, and huge potential for building brand new towns and cities. Plus the occasional skirmish with Apache Indians on horseback, and a bar brawl and gunfight or two along the way.

In other words, there was a time when pretty much everything I thought I knew about North America, was based upon fiction. This was primarily due to the many long-running TV series such as the 'Lone Ranger' and 'Cheyenne', and the Wild West movies like 'Shane' and 'True Grit'.

My boyhood belief had no real basis in reality however, for the historical cowboy led a gruelling life full of hard labour. Most died at a young age.

Like most kids of similar age at the time, playing "Cowboys and Indians" out in the fields and the woods,was great fun. Back then as kids, we made simple bow and arrows, from slender branches cut from hedgerows with penknives; and lengths of string, sneaked from mum's kitchen cupboard more often than not.

Even designer clothing was different back then. In the main it consisted of woollen jumpers, hand-knitted by Grandma, and non-matching, material patches, sewn onto the knees of our trousers.

We also had a regular TV show called "Out of town" with Jack Hargreaves. Jack was an old bearded man with an amiable nature, who always wore a battered hat and was rarely seen without a pipe in his mouth. He showed us how to enjoy traditional rural life, the correct way to bait a fishing hook, and how to plant a garden etc.

The same is true to a large degree, concerning what I thought I knew about the Victorian era. My understanding of that period of English history, was largely based upon Charles Dickens novels, and subsequent movies, such as 'Great Expectations', 'Bleak House' and

'Oliver Twist'.

It did sink in however, that during the Victorian era, there did seem to be a large number of waifs and strays, adult asylums, juvenile asylums, workhouses, poorhouses, alms houses and so forth. But until more recently, I had never stopped to wonder the reason why? I had long acknowledged the fact, but had always taken it for granted; an experience common to most, I guess?

The truth is, we have all been educated and thoroughly indoctrinated in false information, to the point where most don't question what they are told.

From time to time we are presented with 'historical facts' or stumble across something which appears to be somewhat out of the ordinary, and with no given reason as to why. At this point it's all too easy to shrug the matter off, and think little, or no more of it.

For once we start thinking about some of these anomalies more deeply and logically, we are slowly drawn towards a somewhat daunting conclusion. For whatever the reason, and from a relatively young age, we have been spoon-fed a concoction of truth, half truth, deception and outright lies.

Our parents, school teachers and tutors are not to blame for this. They too were indoctrinated from a young age, and only taught their children what they believed to be true, and done so in good faith. Those responsible are and always have been, the controllers of the narrative.

Magic City.

Founded in March, 1882, Billings, Montana, was formed by the Railroad as a western railhead for its further westward expansion. According to Wikipedia and other sources, at first the town only had three buildings, but within just a few months the number had grown to over 2,000. Hence Billings was nicknamed the 'Magic City' because, just like magic, the original 3 house hamlet seemingly became a city overnight. A genuine mistake in the narrative? Or a veiled admission that something else was going on?

A whole load of half buried buildings which already existed maybe? Old world structures which were merely reclaimed and *inherited* by the Railroad company?

Interestingly, the Pictograph Caves are about five miles south of Billings. These caves contain over 100 pictographs (rock paintings), the oldest of which is over 2,000 years old.

Approximately 30,000 artefacts have been excavated from the site, which proved the area has been occupied since at least shortly after Noah's Flood. That would be from around 2600 BC until at least after1800 AD. (*Credit:National Park Service. July 9, 1964.*)

My question is, why in 1964 AD, would the National Park Service refer to the area as having been occupied until 1800 A.D. or soon thereafter? Why not say the area had been occupied until this very day in 1964? What about the 164 years in between? Was the area not occupied then?

Yet another genuine mistake? Or a veiled admission that a period in the time line has been unaccounted for? Your guess is as good as mine. But there were certainly many strange things going on in the 1800's.

The Royal City

Guelph is a city in Southwestern Ontario, Canada, which due to its high proportion of truly spectacular, Gothic-Revival-style buildings, became known as "The Royal City."

In 1831, according to Wikipedia, the village of 'Guelph' had around 800 residents. An industrial watermill and a sawmill were erected in 1832 and 1833 respectively.

The *Smith's Canadian Gazetteer* of 1846, indicates that Guelph at that time, had a population of just 1,240 people, mostly from England and Scotland. Yet over the next 50 years they had built an entire city, which in this case, was constructed in true regal fashion.

By 1850, the population had grown to a little over 7,000 people and in 1856 Guelph was incorporated as a town. Yet 6 years earlier, in 1850 they had opened a Public Library, which was part funded by the Carnegie family.

Built with cut stone, and with an elevated wrap-around architrave and decorative cornice, supported on all 4 sides of the building by rows of Corinthian columns, photos of this construction are a marvel to behold. At the same time, it does raise a serious question.

Why invest so much time, effort and money, into building such an elaborate structure, just to house a large collection of books, on behalf of such a relatively small population of 7,000 people?

Did they really need this vast amount of literature held in such an extravagant building at the time? Or was this grand building a pre-existing structure, inherited and repurposed as a Library? It was demolished in 1964.

For all his benevolent work and monetary donations to society, it's worth remembering, that Andrew Carnegie was instrumental in introducing a transformational change in education.

Was he one of the controllers of history? Most likely, yes.

Other architectural wonders built with cut stone, concrete, brick and marble over this period included the Old Guelph City Hall, the elegant Winter Building, the impressive County Gaol and the grand Georgian-style Governor's residence.

The super-builder

Born in Limerick, Ireland in 1842, Joseph Connolly trained as an architect in Europe, before returning to Dublin in 1871 to form his own practise. Shortly thereafter, Connolly moved to Toronto, Canada, and completed an incredible 21 cathedrals before finally falling off a ladder, and meeting his demise, at the age of 64.

There appear to be no photographs or portraits of this man. But assuming he moved to Canada at the age of 20, Joseph Connolly was able to build almost an entire cathedral each year for the rest of his life. In his spare time we're told by Wikipedia that Connolly;

"also produced some industrial and residential buildings."

What an incredible man! Here is the list of Joseph Connolly's achievements according to the official narrative.

- St. John the Evangelist Church, Arthur, Ontario-1874.
- Church of the Immaculate Conception. Formosa, Ontario-1875.
- St. Patrick's Roman Catholic Church, Hamilton, Ontario-1875.
- St. Peter Church. Ayton, Ontario-1876.
- Basilica of Our Lady Immaculate. Guelph, Ontario. 1877-1926. (Connolly fell from a ladder and died of bronchial asthma 20 years prior to completion.)
- St.Peter's Cathedral Basilica. London, Ontario-1877-1926.
- St. Joseph's Church. Macton, Ontario-1878.
- James Street Baptist Church. Hamilton, Ontario-1879.
- St. Mary's Roman Catholic Church. Toronto, Ontario-1881-1905.
- St. Mary's Pro-Cathedral. Sault Ste.Marie, Michigan.-1881.
- St. Patrick's Church, Kinkora, Ontario-1882.
- Holy Cross Church (now Église Sacré-Coeur) Georgetown, Ontario-1885.

- St. Basil's Church addition. Toronto, Ontario-1886.
- St. Joseph's Church, Chatham, Ontario-1886.
- St. Mary's Cathedral enlargement. Kingston, Ontario-1889.
- Holy Cross Roman Catholic Church. Kemptville, Ontario-1889.
- St. Paul's Basilica. Toronto, Ontario-1889.
- St. Michael's Cathedral redecoration and alterations. Toronto, Ontario-1890.
- St. Paul's Church. Dornoch, Ontario-1890.
- St. John the Evangelist Roman Catholic Church Gananoque, Ontario-1891.
- St. Gregory the Great Roman Catholic Church Picton, Ontario-1892.
- Church of the Good Thief, Kingston, Ontario-1892.

With towers, spires, antennae, domed-rotundas and precision carved ornamentation and rose windows, each building is architecturally stunning in its own unique way. One only has to take a careful and thoughtful look at the photographs of these incredible buildings, to realise how impossible it would have been to construct them all in the time period and manner we are told.

Whilst it cannot be proven of course, yet again the historical record is obviously a fabricated one. To build such amazing and complex structures at the rate of virtually one cathedral per year, would be an impossible task today. Even with the modern machinery, power tools and other specialist equipment we have at our disposal.

The lack of credibility in the official narrative is striking. Why then, would the controllers go to such lengths to fabricate (at least in part) the early construction history of a Canadian city? As far as I can fathom, there would be no financial, political or economic gain. Nor any other incentive for them to do so.

So, if there is nothing to gain by falsifying history, is it possible for something to be lost, by tampering with history?

Yes, in one sense something was lost. For by squeezing, or including far more than is physically possible to achieve, into a given period, effectively reduces the timeline.

In this particular case, we are told that 21 cathedrals were built during an 18 year period between 1874 and 1892. And that's without taking into account, all the other building and construction work going on during the same period.

For at the same time, Wikipedia tells us that the residential and commercial infrastructure of the city was well underway. New railway lines were being constructed to connect with the Great Western Railway, and gas pipes were being laid by the Guelph Gas Company.

There is also another possible reason for fabricating Canada's early history.

From 1815 to 1850, over 800,000 immigrants arrived in Canada, chiefly from the British Isles. Upon arrival, did these early settlers discover a whole load of buildings that should not have been there? Architectural wonders, inherited from the old world? Majestic buildings fit for a Royal City, and far beyond their own ability to construct?

Did the controllers concoct a cover story to justify their existence? Is this why they crammed the construction of as many buildings as possible, into an impossible period of time?

Did Joseph Connolly even exist? Or was he a fictional character invented by the controllers, and slotted into Canadian history to explain the presence of so many wondrous buildings that by rights, should not have been there? Or is this all a strange coincidence?

Yes, it could indeed be considered a strange coincidence, but only if such anomalies were restricted to Canada. Instead, a similar pattern can be found in every city across every nation on earth. For every nation has its own equivalent of a 'Royal City'.

Old photographs of Rio de Janeiro circa 1890 for example, with half empty streets, and the few pedestrians who are present are dwarfed by the towering infrastructure around them. In fact, one gets the distinct impression that the glorious, perfect oversized architecture and the people are not compatible .

Rather than build them, at some point in time, the new residents of Rio de Janeiro who had moved to the city, had *inherited* these incredible old world structures.

In fact, when using a magnifying glass to look more closely at some early photographs of London, Paris and New York, supposedly taken around 1920, it almost appears that telegraph poles, wires, and in some instances, pedestrians and horse-drawn carts, have been superimposed onto them. If this is the case, then we cannot even be certain if the photo was actually taken in the year we are told.

Things that make you go Hmmm

Jon Levi Productions have several documentaries on YouTube exploring the partial ruins of many of the large masonry structures which are found in a number of American states. There appears little or no difference between these ruins and the monumental ruins seen at the ancient site of Pompeii. Why?

I recently watched a short documentary about the Erie Canal in America, in which the producer and narrator raised some interesting but pertinent questions. For this canal could not possibly have been constructed within the time period and in the manner we are told. Reasoning and the use of logic is all that's required to see through the glaring holes in the official narrative.

The original canal was 363 miles long, running from the Hudson River at Albany to Lake Erie in Buffalo. We're told its construction began in 1817, and it opened 8 years later on October 26, 1825. The channel was dug with pick and shovel, plow and scraper, 40 feet wide and 4 feet deep, with removed soil piled on the downhill side to form a towpath.

363 miles over 8 years equates to 45.375 miles per year, or one mile every 8 days. Seriously? Being conservative by assuming all the dirt was dry, approximately 31,288 cubic yards weighing a little over 32,000 tons was excavated every 8 days? 4,000 tons each day? Without the use of automated machinery and only small rectangular carts hauled by oxen or mules, which were limited to a 250-pound load?

Are you starting to get the picture here? Yes, I know, it's an impossible one. And that's just the excavation work, for the sides of the canal were then lined with stone set in clay, and the bottom was also lined with clay.

It wasn't just the mammoth task of digging each day, that the early settlers had to contend with, They also had to fell hundreds of trees as they passed through swathes of virgin forest. They constructed 32 complicated aqueducts, one being 950 feet long to span an 800 foot river, as well as building 34 complex, numbered lock systems.

They also had to pass through the Niagara escarpment, an 80 foot wall of hard limestone, necessitating the building of five locks along a 3-mile corridor to carry the canal over the escarpment. To achieve this they used black, or gun powder, the earliest known chemical explosive, to blast through the rock, as dynamite was not yet invented.

Can anyone seriously believe the official mainstream narrative? Could it be that the early settlers merely inherited this incredible feat of engineering from its previous and unknown constructors? That having taken the credit for it, the "official" narrative is the best the controllers of world history could come up with?

In fact, it's highly likely that the world's entire canal construction narrative has been fabricated. We certainly have the ability to construct waterways, magnificent buildings and highly elaborate architecture, but the timeline many were supposedly built in i.e. during, or barely beyond the horse and cart era, just doesn't add up or make sense.

Now You See Me Now You Don't

A big puzzle is, why so many of the cities monumental structures in North America were razed to the ground and repurposed just a few decades after they were completed.

Was it an effort to hide evidence of the constructional ability of a previous advanced civilization? If so, who exactly were the original builders of these remarkable and in many cases, almost impossible structures?

Completed in 1910, Manhattan's historic Pennsylvania Station or Penn Station enabled direct rail access to New York City from the south for the first time. Its head house and train shed were considered a masterpiece of the Beaux-Arts style and one of the great architectural works of New York City. The station contained 11 platforms serving 21 tracks, in approximately the same layout as the current Penn Station.

This magnificent station was originally constructed on 8 acres of land, and was a half a mile long sitting on two whole city blocks.

Described as a neoclassical masterpiece of elegant, pink granite marble columns, and massive arched-glass windows, the structure was made of 490,000 cubic feet of pink granite, 60,000 cubic feet of interior stone, 27,000 tons of steel, 48,000 tons of brick, and 30,000 light bulbs. *(Credit:Wikipedia.)* The pink granite alone weighed around 24,500 Tons. And this during a time of blocks, pulleys, ropes and chains, and the earliest steam powered locomotive crane with lattice boom. At its completion, the New York Times *(August 29, 1910)* called it "the largest building in the world ever built at one time."

Inspired by Roman architecture, the expansive waiting room, which spanned Penn Station's entire length contained traveller amenities such as long benches, men's and women's smoking lounges, newspaper stands, telephone and telegraph booths, and baggage windows. The waiting room itself measured 314 feet 4 inches (95.81 m) long, 108 feet 8 inches (33.12m) wide, and 150 feet (46m) tall. Additional waiting rooms for men and women, each measuring 100 feet by 58 feet (30m by 18m), were on either side of the main waiting room.

The ceiling was supported by massive Corinthian columns, set on pedestals, each measuring 59.5 feet (18.1 m) tall from the tops of the pedestals to the tops of the capitals There were three semicircular windows on top of the waiting room's walls; each had a radius of 38 feet 4 inches (11.68.m) *[Credit Wikipedia]*

Little wonder historian Jill Jonnes called the original edifice a *"great Doric temple to transportation"*, whilst others described the station as;

"grand a corporate statement in stone, glass and sculpture as one could imagine."

And there it stood, in all its glory, until it was torn down due to multiple train cancellations, a foul smell, and many false rumours 50 years after completion.

At the time it was said;

"One entered the city like a god; one scuttles in now like a rat."

At which point, one also begins to smell a rat. Land purchases for the station started in 1901, a mere two years since Alexander Winton from Cleveland, Ohio, sold his first manufactured semi-truck in 1899. Not sure about you, but personally I think 2 years is cutting it a bit fine for the logistics of the mammoth transportation project that lay ahead.

500 buildings had to be demolished to make way for the station, and a $5 million contract to excavate the site was duly awarded in 1903. We are left to wonder on the size and the architectural style of the 500 destroyed buildings?

Over 3,000,000 cubic yards (2,300,000m^3) of dirt was excavated during construction, which if my calculation is correct equates to 4,500,000 imperial tons. Imagine how many Irish settlers armed with picks and shovels, it took to shift four and a half million tons of dirt and debris by horse and cart.

Whilst a few colour *depictions* (artist impressions) of the original excavation site can be found online, I've been unable to find any images of the excavation work in progress.

The fact this incredible feat of architecture once stood in New York is not in question. But it's hard to find evidence that it was constructed as per the official record states. For there is no way of telling from the available photographs, whether they were taken during its construction, or during the demolition process.

Even if it were built at the time we're told, the loss of this magnificent structure after just a few decades, like many others to boot, seems both unnecessary and even quite sad.

Ada Louise Huxtable wrote in the New York Times in 1963;

> The tragedy is that our present age not only could not produce
> such a building, but could not even maintain it

It would seem Ms. Huxtable also smelt a rat, and realized the impossibility of the official narrative. A building that could not be constructed in "our present age", let alone be maintained.

Hard to believe, but the majestic structure known as Penn Station, like many other remarkable buildings across America and Europe, was more likely an *inherited*, renovated and redesignated structure that was already there, having originally been constructed at an earlier date in the old world?

The official narrative surrounding the construction of New York's Hudson Terminal, is equally dubious. Designed in the Romanesque Revival style, and built during 1908-1909, this incredible structure also included two 22-storey office skyscrapers and three basement levels. Yet another architectural wonder that was demolished a little over 60 years later, in 1971-72.

According to the official narrative, excavations at the site of the office tower buildings were underway by early 1907, and the first columns for the substructure were placed in May, 1907.

Eleven months later, on April 4, 1908, tenants started moving into the towers. The station itself opened the following year on July 19,

1909. A little over two years to construct this huge and elaborate rail terminus which included two 22-storey towers?

I really don't think so!

Construction began on Manhattan's 47-floor Singer Building in 1897, and built in multiple stages it was completed in 1908. The building's architecture was once again visually stunning, containing elements of the Beaux-Arts and French Second Empire styles.

Why was it razed to the ground 60 years later in 1968?

We are told that the asymmetrical L-shaped 26-storey City Investing Building, which was capped by a seven-story central portion with gable roofs, took only 2 years to complete. One only has to look at the available photographs to see this would have been an impossible feat.

Building started in 1906, and it opened in 1908 with about 12 acres (520,000 sq ft) of floor area, becoming one of New York City's largest office buildings at the time.

Just like the Singer Building, the City Investing Building was completely demolished 60 years later, in 1968.

With construction beginning in 1896, and completion in 1897, the 273 feet tall Gillender Building fared far worse by comparison.

With 20 storeys (comprising 17 floors in the main bulk and three floors in a cupola atop the capitol), this building proudly stood in the Financial District of Manhattan, New York, for merely 13 years before its destruction in 1910.

Maybe this was due to a 20-storey building with a rentable floor space area of 37,000 square feet, being constructed in a single year?

This supposed historical "fact" recorded by Wikipedia and most other sources is unbelievable, and little more than a Fairy Tale.

So what was really going on at the time?

Could it be that too many people were starting to ask some difficult questions? Was it easier to demolish many of these buildings, rather than provide realistic answers? For it would be impossible to justify the construction of a highly elaborate 20-storey building over a 12 month period.

An Enigma

In more recent years, construction of the 1,500 feet high John Hancock Center began in 1965 and was completed 4 years later in

1969.

Construction of the 1,450-foot Willis (Sears) Tower, began in 1970 and was completed 4 years later in 1974.

Construction of the 26-storey Skyline Plaza condominium building in Fairfax County, Virginia, began in early 1970, and was due to open three and a half years later in August 1973. Sadly the building collapsed in March, 1973, killing 14 workmen and injuring many more.

Construction on The Shard, a 72-storey building in London, began in March 2009. It was completed a little over 3.5 years later in November 2012.

Standing at 1,550 feet, construction began on Central Park Tower on September 17, 2014. It was completed 5 years to the day later, on September 17, 2019.

Construction of the 1,066 feet Brooklyn Tower began in 2018, with estimated completion 4 years later in 2022.

I've never worked in the construction industry, but these buildings are all unique and require engineering based on their design and soil conditions. I doubt the length of time it takes to build them can be reasonably estimated without any parameters or conditions.

Nevertheless, from the few examples listed above, I think it can be fairly well established, that the minimum amount of time it takes to build a skyscraper today, ranges from three and a half years, to five years. Some take even longer I believe, but let's say that on average, it takes 4 years per building. Bear in mind too, that most work today, is still performed manually and on site.

That said, now let's go back in time.

Construction began on the 792 feet, 60-storey Woolworth Building in New York City 110 years ago, on November 4, 1910. It was completed within a mere 20 months, on July 1, 1912.

Ninety years ago, or so we're told, the construction began of the magnificent, 1,454 feet, 102-storey, Art Deco-style Empire State Building, on March 17, 1930. It was miraculously completed within a mere 13 months, on April 11, 1931.

(This 13 month quick-build hoax, is recorded as historical fact by Wikipedia, Britannica and most other sources).

"Onlookers were enraptured by the sheer height at which the steelworkers operated", we're told, and New York Magazine wrote of the steelworkers:

"Like little spiders they toiled, spinning a fabric of steel against the sky" *(Credit:Wikipedia.)*

Work on the 640 foot tall, 50-storey, General Electric Building commenced on May 3, 1930. It was completed about 18 months later at the end of 1931.

Construction of the 1,046 feet tall, 77-storey Art Deco-style Chrysler Building, took a little longer. It was completed over a 20 month period from September, 1928, to May, 1930.

The 927-foot-tall, Neo-Gothic style, 62-floor Manhattan Company Building (40 Wall Street), tops them all however. Construction began in May 1929, and the building was completed by May 1, 1930, and officially opened on May, 26. (Note the blue copper copper roof, cupola and spire.)

On May 6, 1930, the New York Times headlined;

> Bank of Manhattan Built in Record Time; Structure 927 Feet High, Second Tallest in World, is Erected in Year of Work.

What a sensational headline!

It would be interesting to know what folk reading this thought at the time. Would they have believed the mainstream media without question? In all probability, yes they would, just as I would likely have done if I was living at that time. For we all have a tendency to believe what we read in the newspapers etc. Until we begin to wake up, of course.

In his 1938 book, "Changing the Skyline: An Autobiography" (p.283), Paul Starrett, of the Starrett Corporation, said that;

> Of all the construction work which I have handled, the Bank of Manhattan was the most complicated and the most difficult, and I regard it as the most successful.

I'm sure you're right, Mr. Starrett. Nevertheless, I have just one simple question for you.

How was it possible for you guys to construct a skyscraper 90 years or more ago, in approximately one third of the time it takes today?

Okay, that's a fair point you make, Mr. Starrett. I agree, the average working week back in the 1930's was 50.6 hours, compared with the 37.2 hours in 2019.

But surely, a 13 hour difference in a working week should more than balance out when taking into account, today's more advanced technology, efficient machinery and power tools etc.

What am I missing here, Mr. Starrett? Am I just being illogical? Or are the dates and construction times according to the official narrative flawed, unbelievable and illogical?

Yes, you're absolutely right Mr. Starrett. It is indeed an enigma.

Thanks to the countless hours of diligent research and the dedication of folk such as Ryan Zehm, Jon Levi, Paul Cook and Michelle Gibson etc. in compiling such a remarkable collection of videos and mini documentaries for YouTube, many now believe there was an ulterior motive behind all of this.

The renovation, repurposing or removal of the remaining old world structures, and disguise any traces which would indicate an earlier reset in the timeline. If you think this sounds crazy, then consider this.

Would it be any less crazy, than to believe the Empire State Building was erected at the rate of a fraction under two levels per week? Week in, week out, for 56 weeks straight?

Is there actually any reliable and consistent evidence for the Empire State Building under construction? The answer is no, not really.

While photo and video existed then, we're told that very few photographs survived. The majority of which, show grainy images of a trio of grinning workmen without hard hats or safety harness, sitting astride steel girders, and posing for the camera in a staged, mid-air photo-shoot.

Until a company called EarthCam claimed to have uncovered the long-lost time-lapse footage from 1931, of the entire construction process. A 50- second video which they shared on YouTube.

The date it was uploaded? April 1, 2018.

O why are we so gullible?

Logic and reason scream out, that the official narrative surrounding the Empire State Building, and many other magnificent structures, is a fabricated one. So, when exactly was the Empire State Building constructed? I've no idea. My guess is that it was an *inherited* structure, and was discovered partially buried in the dirt.

Is it possible that from the time of its discovery, the entire area had been cordoned off from the public? Until such time as the building was ready to be displayed in all its glory?

Maybe most of the renovation work was completed in 13 months. But it certainly wasn't built from scratch in 13 months back in 1930.

Do you start to see why many have claimed that our grand cathedrals and other magnificent structures were originally built by aliens from a distant planet, or time travellers from the future? And due to being conditioned by the likes of Hollywood, who can actually blame them?

A fast growing number however, have since rejected the alien and time travel nonsense, and thanks to some mind-blowing research and videos on YouTube etc. now believe the builders were of the Tartarian Empire, which they say once ruled much of the world.

With this I disagree, for as previously mentioned, I cannot believe that any race or nation which has descended from one of the three sons of Noah, has had the ability to build such architectural wonders, or not during the time period we're told, anyway.

Upon saying that, there is a period in European history, generally referred to as 'The Renaissance', covering the 15th and 16th centuries. During this time period, we see a surprisingly rapid, and virtually unexplained increase of a far superior skill and ability, both in architecture and the classical arts in general.

In fact, it would almost appear that the craftsmen and artisans during this remarkable era, were capable of interacting with both the physical realm and the spiritual realm simultaneously.

The basic principles of these buildings were always the same and their quality unrivalled. Each distinctively crafted as though an architecture within an architecture. Is this uniform architecture of such excellent quality, an indication of a unified civilization that no longer exists?

Was the term, 'The Renaissance' merely invented to brush over a remarkable period of history, which in so many different ways is hard to explain? Why did this superior craftsmanship come to a halt? Who were they, and where did these superior craftsmen and artisans go?

We will endeavour to answer this difficult question later.

Raising Cities

I credit the website 'Stolen history'. net for bringing to my attention the bizarre case of elevated cities. And the amazing reconstruction speed of cities destroyed by fire. There were five Great Fires in America just in 1889 alone.

An unusual number of cities were devastated by fire during the nineteenth and early twentieth century, and all had one thing in common. Extensive damage to the city's infrastructure, with minimal loss of life.

Stolen History reports;

- 1842.The Hamburg Fire killed 51people, and destroyed a third of the city, leaving an estimated 20,000 homeless.
- 1845.The Pittsburgh Fire killed 2 people, and destroyed as many as 1,200 buildings.
- 1871.The Chicago Fire killed 122 people, and destroyed 17,500 buildings, 73 miles of road and 120 miles of pavement.
- 1872.The Boston Fire killed 76 people and destroyed 776 buildings.
- 1889.The Seattle Fire killed zero people, and destroyed 2,160 buildings.
- 1889.The Bakersfield Fire killed one person, and destroyed 196 buildings.
- 1901.The Jacksonville Fire killed 7 people, and destroyed 146 city blocks, and more than 2,368 buildings.
- 1916.The Paris, Texas, Fire killed 3 people, and destroyed 1,400 buildings.

That's not to mention the many other great city fires that broke out during the 19th and the 20th centuries. Hundreds, maybe thousands of cities throughout the entire realm have suffered a similar fate.

Hundreds of thousands, possibly millions of city buildings (many of them supposedly wooden) have been destroyed by these fires, and in each case they have been replaced by masonry structures, in a relatively short space of time. Yet strangely enough, there are comparatively few photographs of these new buildings under construction. In fact, they are extremely rare, if they can be found at all.

It's very likely that in many cases false narratives were deployed to disguise what is known as a "controlled burn"; a planned event to destroy and/or repurpose old world structures and to revise history.

Seattle

Blamed on woodworking shop assistant, John Back, for over-heating a pot of glue using a gasoline fire, the Great Seattle Fire of June 6, 1889, blazed for one day only, yet it destroyed approximately 120 acres of the city, including the entire central business district of Seattle. This was due in the main, to virtually all of the structures in the neighbourhood at the time, being wooden. Hence the fire spread rapidly and the majority of buildings were razed to the ground. Yet there were Zero fatalities.

The fire however is not the issue here, but rather the incredible speed at which the city was rebuilt. There is some discrepancy over exactly how many city blocks were destroyed by the fire, with numbers ranging from 45 to 64 blocks. This variation is likely due to some being single blocks, whilst others were double, and may have been counted twice.

Either way, after the Seattle fire there was a new rule enacted, that no more wooden buildings could be constructed, and new building standards and regulations were set. Rather than starting over at another location, Seattle's citizens decided to rebuild on the same site, and by the end of 1890, brand new masonry buildings had been erected in their stead. A total rebuild period of eighteen months.

According to the local news paper, 'The Seattle Post-Intelligencer' dated January 1, 1891,(emphasis mine),

> The conditions of *1889* were extraordinary, and the devastation caused by the fire rendered necessary the immediate construction of a great number of buildings and the outlay of enormous sums of money. Construction *during the year* therefore, reached high water mark, the amazing number of *3,465* new buildings being the result.

The same newspaper of January1, 1891, also reported;

> There were constructed in Seattle and suburbs during 1890, and are in course of construction, *2,100* buildings upon which an aggregate of $8,935,657 was expended.

> It is not too much to say that no other city of 50,000 inhabitants in the United States can make such a remarkable showing of great rows of business blocks constructed in the most artistic,

costly, and expensive manner.

Bear in mind these are documented "facts" from January1, 1891, which refer to the years 1889-1890. Over the two year period, we are told that a grand total of 5,625 new buildings were erected, 2,100 of which were still under construction. Hence, 3,465 new buildings were constructed over an 18 month period.

If 3,465 new buildings is correct, that amounts to 192.5 buildings a month, or 6.4 buildings per day, with no days, and no nights off. And this, without taking into account, clearing up all the ash, debris and mess left behind in the wake of the fire.

Nowhere are we told what percentage of Seattle's 50,00 inhabitants were children, nor told how many brick layers and masons came to rebuild Seattle. One way or another it had to be enough to erect 6.4 buildings a day in 1890.

We're not talking about erecting quick-build housing estates, although many were one-to-two storey frame buildings, mostly for single-family homes. But most were designed in the Richardsonian Romanesque style, which incorporates 11th and 12th century southern French, Spanish, and Italian characteristics.

 Others were massive, beautiful and complex, such as the 7-storey Seattle-Harrisburg Building, the 6-storey Hotel Seattle and the 6-storey Pioneer Building, to name but a few.

The architectural design of these buildings is truly impressive, each having amazing stonework and hundreds of windows, and although not a builder myself, I suspect each building alone, would have taken far longer than 18 months to complete. More like a minimum of 2 or 3 years per building at a guess.

Where these 3,465 buildings originally came from, or who built them in the first place, I really wouldn't know. But 3,465 buildings certainly weren't constructed over an 18 month period, as the official narrative claims.

It's even hard to tell from the available photographs, whether or not the larger and more elaborate buildings were actually new at the time the photo was taken. Indeed, some appear to be fairly old and well weathered, rather than a spanking brand new building.

Where did all the new building material come from? The millions of bricks for example, required to rebuild Seattle? At the time, Seattle was famous for its Henry Yesler's sawmill, but that's about it.

Under the heading; *A Family Owned Northwest Company*, 'Mutual Materials' claim;

> As a local family owned and operated company with fifth-generation family leadership, Mutual Materials was founded in *1900* by Daniel Houlahan as Builders Brick Company. Following the Great Seattle Fire of *1890*, our brick literally rebuilt Seattle and can be seen in many historic buildings today.

This is just one of multiple discrepancies which appear in the narrative. The Seattle Fire occurred in June 1889, not 1890, and Houlahan we're told, whose "brick literally rebuilt Seattle" founded a brick factory at the base of Beacon Hill in *1900*. That's a minimum of ten years *after* the fire.

Assuming Mutual Materials made a genuine mistake, and the Builders Brick Company built a factory in 1889, the year of the fire, one then has to account for the time it took to build the plant, before production could even begin. I'm sure that building a brick making factory from scratch in 1889 was no mean task.

Yet we're told from June 6, 1889, that **3,465** new buildings were erected in 18 months, bringing us to 1891. How did a 19th century brick making plant, produce enough bricks to construct a minimum of four buildings per day, for 18 months straight?

Compared to automated mass production plants today, brick manufacturing in the 1800's was a far more labour intensive and lengthy process.

It's easy enough to find the information about brick production at the time, which was likely to be a maximum of 36,000 bricks per week. The approximate number of bricks that are required to build three 4-bedroom houses.

Something is not right with the official narrative, although I'm not entirely sure in which way. Were these alleged new buildings actually constructed in 1889? Or was the fire itself used as an excuse to excavate and renovate buildings from the old world, buildings that already existed?

It's hard to tell from the scenery in the available photographs, which is an actual construction zone, and which might be an excavation or demolition work in progress. But there was certainly something very bizarre going on in Seattle at the time. And now the story gets even stranger.

According to Wikipedia; "Seattle quickly rebuilt using brick and stone buildings that sat 20 feet (6.1m) *above* the original street level". Other sources confirm the same. All the new buildings constructed in Seattle after the fire, sat a minimum of 20 feet *above* the original street level.

'University Libraries' (Washington) inform us that;

"At the same time, streets were raised up to 22 feet in places, helping to level the hilly city."

What does that even mean? Did thousands of workmen physically shift mountains of dirt to fill in the valleys and troughs between the hills, in order to level the entire area?

Actually, yes, that's exactly what they did, according to the narrative anyway. Hosepipes and thousands of gallons of water, were used to sluice the topsoil from the side of the hills, and somehow they managed to steer the flow of sodden earth downhill to the required location. Exactly how they managed to achieve this remarkable feat, we are not told.

Maybe this all sounds quite plausible when taking a quick glance at the narrative. But is it really? For when giving more thought to what they would have us believe, questions begin to arise, and the official narrative starts to crumble.

Can you imagine the sheer volume, and the enormous tonnage of ballast and dirt required, to raise the entire area of the rebuilt city 20 feet above its original level? I would love to know what construction and excavation equipment they had at the time, to achieve all this. As far as I can find, the most innovative form of machinery for this type of work, was the old fashioned Steam Shovel.

There's no disputing that the original neighbourhood of Seattle was completely gutted, and was either destroyed accidentally, or was intentionally demolished by fire. Nor is it disputed that the ground level across the entire area, underwent a radical change of some sort. Evidently tourists can still pay a fee to visit a network of underground passageways and basements in the Pioneer Square area, which we're told, was the original ground level of the city.

The problem is, after having been told the original buildings were virtually all made of wood, when viewing photographs of the Seattle underground, all we see are the remains of concrete and brick built structures. And so, yet again the official storyline crumbles.

According to the narrative, when they reconstructed their buildings, merchants and landlords knew that the original ground floor would eventually be underground and the next floor, twenty feet above, would be the new ground floor.

We're even told that during the construction process, rather than walk up the street, around the corner and along the foot path, pedestrians had to climb 20-foot ladders to access the new level above.

Can we really believe that elderly customers with a bagful of shopping had to scramble down a twenty foot ladder to get back home? If this crazy story makes little sense, it is because we are not being told the truth.

What puzzles me, is why go to such extreme measures to raise the entire area by a minimum of 20 feet, without bothering to demolish the original ground level infrastructure first? Or at the very least fill everything in.

Was the whole event a fabricated cover story, used to explain away the evidence for scores of old world structures, found buried or partially buried beneath the ground? The majority of which were fully excavated and renovated, to produce the new Seattle? If so, it's quite remarkable how they got away with it.

Something very strange was going on during the nineteenth century that we have little or no knowledge of, due to fabricated stories like this one. And how about the bogus story of the entire City of Chicago being raised by at least six feet?

Chicago

During the 19th century, the elevation of the Chicago area was little higher than the shoreline of Lake Michigan, so for many years, there was little or no naturally occurring drainage from the city surface. The lack of drainage caused unpleasant living conditions, and standing water harboured pathogens that caused numerous epidemics including typhoid fever and dysentery, which blighted Chicago six years in a row, culminating in the 1854 outbreak of cholera that killed around six percent of the city's population. (Credit:Wikipedia).

In 1856, engineer Ellis S. Chesbrough, drafted a plan for the installation of a citywide sewerage system and submitted it to the Common Council, which adopted the plan.

One major problem, much of the city was built on marshland. To overcome this, and make room for the new sewers, workers first laid drains and refinished and covered the roads and the pavements with up to 6 feet of soil.

Can you imagine the mountains of rubble and dirt needed to raise the new street level of an entire city by 6 feet? And this gargantuan task carried out 30 years or so before the sale of the first semi-truck? In March 1862, the Chicago Tribune observed;

"Chicago is deep in mud. Mud floats in the atmosphere — we have mud on the sidewalks, on streets, on bridges, in fact, m-u-d is written everywhere in unmistakable characters."

But by increasing the height of the streets, suddenly the buildings around them would be either part-buried, or several feet lower, meaning a flight of steps would be required, running from the new street level, down to the building's entrance. To get around this problem, the planners came up with the ingenious idea of raising the entire city centre's brick-built structures by an average of 6 feet instead.

According to Wikipedia; "The work was funded by private property owners and public funds." Wikipedia also tells us;

> In January 1858, the first masonry building in Chicago to be thus raised—a four-story, 70-foot (21m) long, 750-ton (680 metric tons) brick structure situated at the north-east corner of Randolph Street and Dearborn Street—was lifted on two hundred jackscrews to its new grade, which was 6 feet 2 inches (1.88m) higher than the old one, "without the slightest injury to the building." It was the first of more than fifty comparably large masonry buildings to be raised that year.

To achieve this truly mammoth undertaking, teams of construction engineers physically raised most of the city's buildings to the new level by using multiple rows of jack-screws and hydraulic jacks.

The official narrative tells us that once raised by six feet, and whilst supported in mid air by dozens of hydraulic jacks, new foundation walls were quickly erected in the 6 foot gap beneath the building. Furthermore, businesses operating in the premises remained open during the entire process.

Without batting an eyelid, people seemingly came and went, done their shopping, or worked in them as if nothing out of the ordinary were happening.

'Enjoy Illinois' website states;

> Eventually, they even figured out how to raise an entire block at
> once. They placed 6,000 jackscrews under the one-acre block
> between Lake, Clark and LaSalle streets, estimated at 35,000
> tons in weight, and raised the whole thing over four days—
> buildings, sidewalks and all. The process was gradual enough
> that business continued in the buildings throughout.

Many buildings were even larger, the Tremont House Hotel for
example. This luxurious, brick-built building which had a footprint
of over one acre, stood six storeys high. It remained open for
business throughout the operation, or so we're told.
According to 'Living History of Illinois and Chicago'®

> One patron was puzzled to note that the front steps leading from
> the street into the hotel were becoming steeper every day and
> that when he checked out, the windows were several feet above
> his head, whereas before they had been at eye level. This huge
> hotel, which until just the previous year had been the tallest
> building in Chicago, was in fact raised fully 6 feet without a
> hitch.

This is utterly nonsensical if one stops to think about what is being
said here. For we're told that each building was raised by six feet,
complete and intact without any damage to the structure. The
surrounding streets and pavements were also raised by six feet
accordingly.
In other words, both the building and the infrastructure surrounding
it were all raised by the same amount of six feet Hence both still
remained more or less at the same level. Flights of steps leading
from the pavement up to the hotel entrance would *not* become
steeper. And windows would *not* rise by several feet, but remain at
eye level.
Can you not see how the entire mainstream narrative has been
fabricated? The million dollar question is why? What are they trying
to hide?
Not every building went through the raising process, because many
were wooden. These old wooden buildings were placed onto rollers,
and drawn by horses, were moved to the outskirts of town.
We're even told that many enterprising owners of businesses
operating in these wooden buildings continued to serve customers,
even as the buildings were rolling down the street.

Talk about doing a shopping run!

According to *Wikipedia,* Scottish salesman, David Macrae, who was in Chicago on business at the time, wrote,

> Never a day passed during my stay in the city that I did not meet one or more houses shifting their quarters. One day I met nine. Going out Great Madison Street in the horse cars we had to stop twice to let houses get across.

Whatever might have been going on at the time, and for whatever reason, the entire story is at best, a fabricated one. Although there is some photographic evidence of huge buildings suspended above ground level and supported by rows of hydraulic jacks, it is certainly not conclusive.

For there is no way of knowing whether or not each building was actually being raised by six feet. Indeed, it's equally possible that six feet of mud and dirt had accumulated around the building itself, and was being systematically removed.

Put another way, several feet of soil was excavated from around a partially buried old world building, making it now appear to stand on a higher level. Was this the true purpose behind the supposed elevating of entire cities? Your guess is as good as mine, but either way, we've all been hoodwinked.

Theoretical I know, but as I said previously, we're not privy to the knowledge of what was really going on in the 1800's. What happened? When did it happen? Or did it even happen at all? One way or the other, this entire bizarre event, like so many others could be classified as a historical anomaly.

If raising cities was so achievable in the nineteenth century, why aren't we doing it any more? Rather than raising cities, the controllers are more intent on razing cities.

The Great Fire

Twelve years after the city was miraculously raised by six feet, the Great Chicago Fire of October 8-10, 1871, killed approximately 300 people, destroyed roughly 3.3 square miles of the city including over 17,000 structures, and left more than 100,000 residents homeless.

The fire, (which was blamed on Mrs O'Leary's cow for knocking over a lantern) also raises questions. For the narrative suggests that 40 years previous, most if not all of the buildings raised to the new level, were brick built. And how the wooden structures were rolled down the streets and removed to the outskirts of town.

In other words, we are given the distinct impression that back in the 1860's when the city and its streets were raised, by far the majority of the buildings were of masonry construction.

Yet Wikipedia tell us that;

> More than two-thirds of the structures in Chicago at the time of the fire were made entirely of wood, with most of the houses and buildings being topped with highly flammable tar or shingle roofs. All of the city's sidewalks and many roads were also made of wood.

However, when checking out the schematic diagrams of Chicago, which were drawn *prior* to the great fire, it's hard to tell exactly which wooden buildings Wikipedia are referring to. For virtually every building in the diagram is depicted as being a masonry structure. The majority being 3-storey and 4-storey, multi-windowed, flat-roofed buildings.

A lithographic view of the original Chicago City Hall, (created in April, 1866, by Louis Kurz), is a classic example. A towering, 5-storey, old world masonry building, complete with domed rotunda and spiked antenna. Yet we are expected to believe this architectural wonder, was built by the very people we see in the street. Those whose only means of transport at the time, was the horse and cart that we see with them.

At the same time, we are led to believe that the main reason why the old city hall and the buildings surrounding it, were destroyed in the great fire, is because they were primarily constructed from wood?

Any who are inclined to research the architecture of Chicago in 1868, might be in for quite a surprise.

Likewise, photographs taken in the aftermath of the great fire, hold more than a few surprises. Not in the least, because we are told that primarily wooden buildings were destroyed in the blaze.

Yet most of the images show the remnants of concrete, brick and mortar structures supposedly destroyed by fire, yet without any real trace of extensive fire damage. Furthermore, the ruins look strangely clean. There is no soot, no charred and half burnt wooden beams, no flame-blackened windows, no sodden remains of blankets, furniture, carpet, rugs, clothing etc. Only rubble.

In fact, it almost appears as if these buildings were destroyed by some form of explosive weaponry, or laser technology way ahead of its time, that we're totally unaware of.

What type of fire can split large concrete blocks, reduce masonry buildings to single bricks, rubble and dust, whilst nearby trees and wooden Telegraph poles remained barely untouched? One particular photograph has three large, upright concrete blocks, each split or cut vertically down the middle.

In fact these images are uncannily reminiscent of photographs taken in more recent times. The strange wildfires that mysteriously broke out in California in 2015 and 2017 for example. Here we see entire rows of houses turned to dust with very little debris, whilst nearby bushes and pine trees fail to ignite and remain standing untouched.

It's almost as though these fires are selective in what to consume, ignoring Fire Breaks, and skipping over one potential fuel source to devour another.

With any fire or other catastrophe on a city-wide scale, there would be millions of tons of brick, concrete, marble and other debris to clean up. Again, apart from a handful of photos of the occasional workman wielding a broom or shovel, and a horse or two hauling a cart of brick rubble, there is virtually zero evidence of a mammoth clear up operation.

In a lengthy article at *National Geographic* for example, there is only one photograph of the actual clean up.

This doesn't prove anything of course, apart from the fact that nobody could be bothered to take pictures of the hundreds, maybe thousands of people clearing the streets. All very strange.

Although the size of the city has since been increased, the rebuilding process, which we're told began the day immediately after the fire, was completed within less than two years. Once again, in record time and with relatively few photographs of this huge undertaking.

Writes Carl Smith, professor emeritus of English at Northwestern University and author of '*Chicago's Great Fire: The Destruction and Resurrection of an Iconic American City*';

> The great legend of Chicago is that it's a 'phoenix city' – it
> almost instantly rebuilt itself bigger and better from the ashes.
> And to a certain and significant extent, that's true.

The reconstructed 10-storey, Chicago City Hall for example, which opened in February 1911, was completed six years before Ford had

produced what may be considered the first pickup truck made in
America — the Ford Model TT, in 1917. Yet another remarkable
achievement during the horse and cart era, wouldn't you say?

Why have there been so many cities destroyed by Fire over the last
400 years? And why was the reconstruction process achieved in
record time? Are these bizarre tales of entire cities being elevated by
up to 20 feet, merely science fiction, to cover up any trace of an epic
world-changing event? One not recorded in our history books?

Or was the entire city-raising narrative invented, in an attempt to
justify the existence of the architectural evidence for an earlier
advanced civilization. Followed by a Great City Fire, which then
justified the destruction of that evidence?

There are several old maps that clearly show the name Chilaga in
roughly the same location as to where Chicago would be established
200 years later. In the 1890s, a Newspaper Article from the Chicago
Tribune covered this topic, but 6 days later a response was issued in
order to downplay and debunk it.

Could this have been because they didn't want folk to know that
Chicago is actually much older, and was established by an earlier
people, and *not* by the European settlers in the 1800s?

Helen H. Tanner *(1916-2011)* who was a distinguished scholar of
American Indian history, and a former research associate at the
Newberry Library of Chicago, once said;

"Chilaga is a legendary, mythical place that kept cropping up on
early maps."

"It is tops on my list to investigate," she said. "I don't know if you
can say it had a connection with the present-day Chicago."

She further remarked how; "It sometimes turns out, that the
statistically most far out possibility turns out to be the right one."
(reported by the Chicago Tribune Mar 04, 1987.)

Some suspect that the World's Columbian Exposition of 1893, aka
the Chicago World Fair was actually held at the former site of
Chilaga. That the fourteen palatial main buildings, and all the other
supposedly temporary grand structures, already existed as old world
buildings. This of course, would likely to "the statistically most far
out possibility" of them all.

I'm not saying that it's the right one, but it would certainly go a long
way to explain how these majestic and supposedly temporary

buildings were constructed in record time, and why virtually all of them were destroyed the following year.

The official reason being, we are told they were all constructed on a temporary basis from wood, plaster of Paris, hemp fibre and straw.

The temporary Agricultural Building for example, which prior to its destruction, was illuminated at night with a spotlight shining across the lagoon.

Tartaria

On April 24, 1881, The New York Times headline read;

THE RUSSIAN NIHILISTS; THEIR CREED AND WHAT IT MEANS. THE IDENTITY OF NIHILISM WITH TARTARISM--ASIATIC NOMADS SEEKING TO DESTROY WESTERN CIVILIZATION--THE PRESENT CZAR'S DANGER.

The main article continues with;

> "What is Nihilism? What is behind its terrible formula: "Our mission is to destroy all that now exists; the task of the next generation will be to build upon our ruins?" Its acts and declarations are monstrous; humanity condemns, without a dissentient voice, its foul crimes, but even monsters are obedient to a law of some kind."

Like many other parts of the world, America is littered with the footprints of an earlier civilization. A people which in many ways, seem to surpass the technical ability of the earliest American settlers. The 50 State Capitol Buildings of the United States for example, appear to have been constructed far earlier than the official given date of between 1885 and 1900. Not only would they take more than a couple of years to construct (even in the present day) they were also rarely photographed while under construction, and evidently no blue prints are available.

This should come as little or no surprise, considering that all of the US Capitol Buildings, which have domes with rotundas were likely built by the same people, but *inherited* by the new arrivals to America.

That's why some researchers point to a former world empire, of Tartarian origin, that has been erased from our history.

They hold the belief that most architectural styles and technology associated with Western Europe and beyond, actually originated with a people known asTartarians. They had noticed that prior to the 18th and 19th century, many world maps included a region called 'Tartary' or 'Grand Tartary' in the east of Russia, Central Asia and Siberia. Many have questioned why after about 1812, it seems to have been erased from maps as if it did not exist on the face of the earth.

The 1771 Encyclopedia Britannica describes Grande Tartaria as a vast country in the northern parts of Asia, bounded by Siberia on the north and west. Tartary/Tartaria (from the root tartar, meaning savage, barbaric) was a blanket term used in nineteenth century western European literature and cartography, for a vast part of Asia bounded by the Caspian Sea, the Ural Mountains, the Pacific Ocean, and the northern borders of China, India and Persia.

On August 24, 1999, the CIA released a classified 14 page document originally published on June 1, 1957. On page 10 we read;

> Or let us take the matter of history, which, along with religion, language and literature, constitute the core of a people's cultural heritage. Here again the Communists have interfered in a shameless manner. For example on 9 August, 1944, the Central Committee of the Communist Party, sitting in Moscow, issued a directive ordering the party's Tartar Provincial Committee "to proceed to a scientific revision of the history of Tartaria, to liquidate serious shortcomings and mistakes of a nationalistic character committed by individual writers and historians in dealing with Tartar history".
>
> In other words, Tartar history was to be rewritten—let us be frank, was to be falsified—in order to eliminate references to Great Russian aggressions and to hide the facts of the real course of Tartar-Russian relations. And this was no isolated case. In every Muslim area within the USSR, historians, on orders of the Communist Party, have rewritten history to distort the facts so that the Russians always appear in a good light. Needless to say, histories which present the facts truthfully have been withdrawn and destroyed, so that the present and future generations of Muslims are forever denied the chance of learning the true facts of their nations' past.

At this point, it should be noted that the CIA is one of the most corrupt and manipulative organizations in the world. Especially when it comes to creating a major incident, for the sole purpose of pinning the blame for that incident on another individual, group or nation.

Al-Qaeda and Osama Bin Laden for example, who had nothing to do whatsoever, with the attack on New York City, yet in 2001 became the CIA's Scapegoat for the destruction of the Twin Towers. Or creating a major distraction, for the sole purpose of diverting attention elsewhere, that folk should believe a lie. Either way, in 1981 CIA director William J. Casey said;

"We'll Know Our Disinformation Program is Complete When *Everything* the *American* Public *Believes* is False."

One way by which the agency could possibly achieve their goal of total deception, is by releasing previously Top Secret, classified information. In this case pointing the finger at Russia for having falsified or hidden the truth concerning Tartarian history from the public.

For the curious might say, or at least suspect, that if the information was of such a highly sensitive nature, that it had to be kept secret for the last 40 years or so, then surely, it must be true?

"There has to be something concerning the history of Tartaria, that we the public, are not supposed to know", they say. "Hence why the record was falsified, to conceal the truth, and keep us in the dark".

But this is not necessarily the case. It's possible, even quite likely in fact, to be a major distraction, one designed to keep those who ask questions from looking in the right direction for answers. Hence, if there is an answer to be found, invariably it will be the wrong one.

For back in 1999, the year the CIA declassified the document, relatively few folk had even heard of Tartaria, let alone developed an interest in Tartarian history. It's only been in more recent times that interest in Tartaria has grown exponentially.

Who was responsible for keeping this history under wraps? Russia of course! according to the CIA. Personally, I believe "Tartaria" is a cleverly managed PSYOP, a distraction. A fabricated cover story intended to influence a person's objective reasoning and keep them from looking in the right direction.

Many researchers are now saying, the great Tartarian Empire had their own flag and was a multi cultural empire that covered most of the Earth. A civilization so gifted and knowledgable, that they were able to harness the power of electromagnetism directly from the Ionosphere.

Although this remains a theory, for which there is no hard evidence, there are multiple factors, circumstantial, visual or otherwise, which when linked together suggest the theory is likely to be basically true.

In my own personal view however, to refer to this supposed worldwide empire as being Tartarian, is dangerous, for it limits one's perception of what the Old World truly was.

Cathedrals

There are literally thousands of old churches, abbeys, minsters and cathedrals dotted across the United Kingdom, which date back for centuries. It's also alleged that many of these old structures are precisely aligned with Ley lines, also known as telluric or earth currents, a natural electric current flowing on and beneath the surface of the Earth and generally following a direction parallel to the surface.

We are told that while the cathedral foundations were being laid, and under the watchful eye of a Master Quarryman a team of skilled craftsmen produced the blocks of stone that would be used in the building process. The question of how the hundreds of thousand tons of building material arrived at the build site however, is generally avoided.

This should come as no surprise, for if the load is placed in a wheeled cart, a horse can pull 1.5 times its body weight over long distances. For example, a 2,000-pound horse can pull a 3,000-pound cart or a little over 1.5 tons.

Official history tells us that 70,000 tons of stone, 3,000 tons of timber and 450 tons of lead were used in the construction of Salisbury Cathedral. The spire and tower together, which were built at a later date, added an *extra* 6,397 tons to the weight of the building.

The freestone used for the main body of the cathedral came from the Teffont Evias Quarry, about 11 miles away, and it was constructed over a period of 38 years. With a combined total weight of building materials being 73,450 tons, we are left with an approximate 49,000 cartloads. Meaning 1,289 cart loads per year, or 25 cartloads per week, week in week out, over the entire construction period of 38 years.

The additional 6,397 tons of limestone used for the spire and tower, was quarried and transported from Corfe Castle, a distance of 45 miles. More than a 2 day journey, and 6,397 tons of stone being approximately 4,264 cart loads.

Was this achievable in the twelfth century with primitive highways by today's standards? Possibly. But one really doesn't have to be a genius to figure out why information concerning the logistics at the time of construction, is scarce.

Although many church buildings have since been elevated to cathedral status, an emerging theme can be found in the historical record of the original 42 Cathedrals in England.

Most, we are told, were erected on the site of an earlier Norman church or abbey, and construction work began at a time when the local population amounted to little more than a thousand souls. And that's a fairly conservative figure.

In *1377*, the first true poll tax was levied in England, in which everyone over the age of 14 who was not exempt, was required to pay a groat to the Crown. The records taken listed the name and location of everyone who paid the tax, and so gave an excellent measure to estimate the population numbers at the time. Although assumptions need to be made about the proportion of the population who were under 14, generally taken to be around a third.

By 1530 the population of England and Wales had risen to around 3 million and by 1600 it was about 4 million.

The seventeenth and the eighteenth centuries proved a low point for Britain's demography, with no major structured survey of the nation's populations. The best estimate from this period is obtained from the hearth tax of 1662, which formed a survey of the number of hearths in each home.

English historian W. G. Hoskins, records in his 1984 book, 'Local History in England', the population figures for 30 cathedral towns and cities in the year *1377*.

Construction of the 342 feet long, Hereford Cathedral as it stands today, began in 1079. Yet 300 years later in 1377, the population of Hereford was still only 1,903 people.

Construction of the 558 feet long Winchester Cathedral as it stands today, also began in 1079. Yet 300 years later, the population of the city was still only 1,440 people.

At 536 feet in length, construction began on Ely Cathedral in 1083, yet 300 years later the city had a population of just 1,772 people.

With a tower height of 203 feet, construction began on Worcester Cathedral in 1084, yet 300 years later, the city had a mere 1,557 inhabitants.

Construction of the 220 feet tall, Leicester Cathedral began in 1086,

yet a little under 300 years later the population was 2,100 people.
Construction work began on the 225 feet tall, Gloucester Cathedral in 1089, yet around 300 years later, the population was 2,239 people. The six examples listed above, provide a pattern that can be found in the historical record of most all English cathedrals.

If we were to assume a fairly conservative two-fold increase in population growth over this period of 300 years, then construction work on these English cathedrals began when the local population was on average less than 1,000 souls. Approximately one-third of whom, were children under the age of 14, leaving an adult population of around 600. Furthermore, we are led to believe each cathedral was constructed over a relatively short period of time, in some cases just a few decades. Does that even sound plausible to you?

Why were so many cathedrals constructed in England over roughly the same time period? Why would such a relatively small population construct these magnificent and highly complex buildings? Especially at a time when realistically, they lacked the means and ability to do so? Were these grand buildings inherited by the local community, rather than constructed by them?

To help put things into perspective, 700 years *after* the completion of Salisbury Cathedral for example, construction began on Liverpool Cathedral in 1904, with a city population of 685,000 people. Yet *seven* centuries *previous*, and with a population of around 1,000 people, we're told that the main body of Salisbury Cathedral, was completed in 38 years, from 1220 to 1258. The tower and spire alone weigh 6,397 tons, the stone being quarried and transported at a later date from Corfe Castle, 45 miles away.

Even with the rapid advancement of technology during the Industrial Revolution, Liverpool Cathedral took nearly double the length of time, of 74 years to complete. Unlike their predecessors, who 700 years earlier had managed to haul thousands of tons of limestone by horse and cart from a site 45 miles away, Liverpool Cathedral was built mainly of red brick and local sandstone quarried and transported by lorries from the South Liverpool suburb of Woolton.

Could all this strangeness be due to the fact, that unlike the cathedrals built seven hundred years earlier, Liverpool Cathedral was *not* an inherited structure? For there is much verifiable documentation and plenty of photographs showing the cathedral under construction.

Once again, something doesn't seem to sit right with the official narrative. Has it been fabricated, at least in part, by the controllers? In order to cram the construction of as many old cathedrals as possible, into a limited time-frame? A time-frame inhabited by a people without the means and ability to build them? For it seems that at least 800 years of earlier history has been inserted into our present timeline.

Architectural Wonders

The building of monumental cathedrals was never for religious purposes, nor even as an expression of faith by the builders. Religion in the institutional sense was created by the controllers, in order to control the population, and in many cases has been used as a vital tool of deception to justify the old world's infrastructure.

For when viewing these architectural wonders, one clearly sees that those who constructed them did so for a purpose, and possessed a creative ability as good as unrivalled today.

The Milan Cathedral in Italy, we are told, took nearly six hundred years to complete: construction began in 1386, and the final details were completed in 1965. The majestic Cathedral's five broad naves, divided by 40 pillars, are reflected in the hierarchic openings of the façade. Even the transepts have aisles. The nave columns are 280 feet high, and the apsidal windows are 68 by 28 feet.

The huge building is of brick and stone construction, faced with quarried marble. The roof of the cathedral is an amazing forest of openwork pinnacles and spires (antennae) set upon delicate flying buttresses. Some of the finish work is just amazing and even the stone work on the foundations is thought provokingly perfect.

Who prepared the groundwork and excavated the footings back in the fourteenth century? Where did all the concrete come from just to lay a solid foundation beneath this massive building?

The sculpted blocks, the fine marble and granite, the wood, the metals for domes, spires and antennae, the mosaics, the paint finishes, the gold leafing, the sculptures, where did it all come from? The required scaffolding alone would be a logistical nightmare. How were hundreds of thousands of tons of building material transported from their source to the build site?

How was this possible for men with horse and carts, picks, shovels and a collection of modest hand tools, as we are expected to believe? Speak to any builder or structural engineer, and if honest, they'll say; It's not.

Religious icons and stained glass windows may well have been added since the time of Napoleon in the early 1800's. Interestingly, on 20 May 1805, Napoleon Bonaparte, about to be crowned King of Italy, ordered the façade to be finished by architect, Carlo Pellicani. The 46.5 feet, golden Madonnina statue for example, which was designed, built and placed atop a spire by Pellicani, which at 417 feet is the tallest point in Milan.

We are told that Magdeburg Cathedral in Germany was constructed over the period of 300 years starting from 1209, and the completion of the steeples took place only in 1520. Yet the exquisite high-tech stonework and the intricate detail of the metal antennae make us folk today, seem a primitive people by comparison to those who built it.

Is it possible that the Europeans merely inherited this magnificent structure along with all the other colossal works of art?

How about the stunning architecture of the magnificent St. Basil's Cathedral which stands in Moscow's Red Square.

Constructed from red brick and white stone, according to Wikipedia, although the site dates back to the 14th century, the cathedral as it stands today, was built from 1555 to 1561 on orders from Ivan the Terrible. Standing at 151 feet tall, and complete with ornamental, corbelled arches, the cathedral has nine domes arranged in perfect symmetry, each topped with antennae, and each resembling the flame of a bonfire rising into the sky.

In his book, *'Russian Architecture and the West' [p.126]*, Russian historian Dmitry Shvidkovsky, describes it thus.

> It is like no other Russian building. Nothing similar can be found in the entire millennium of Byzantine tradition from the fifth to the fifteenth century, a strangeness that astonishes by its unexpectedness, complexity and dazzling interleaving of the manifold details of its design.

Interestingly, watercolour paintings of the Cathedral and the Red Square by Russian contemporary artist, Fyodor Alexeev, circa 1800, show the adjacent streets covered with a thin layer of mud and dirt. Again, the local residents and their way of life, primitive in comparison to the glorious architecture surrounding them.

What we see in these paintings are two different worlds, each one alien to the other, and portrayed on canvas for all to see. The very notion that folk of this era had the technology and ability to build such massive and beautiful structures, is an incredible, if not impossible one.

One of St. Petersburg's greatest engineering marvels is St. Isaac's Cathedral (now a museum),whose 333 feet tall gilded dome, of more than 100 kilograms of gold, dominates the city skyline.

The exterior is faced with grey and pink stone, and features a total of 112 red granite columns with Corinthian capitals, each hewn and erected as a single block: 48 at ground level, 24 on the rotunda of the uppermost dome, 8 on each of four side domes, and 2 framing each of four windows.

We are told it was built by an army of serfs, who sunk 10,000 tree trunks into the marshy banks and fenlands of the River Neva to support the cathedral's colossal weight of more than 300,000 tons.

In this instance, Wikipedia is a little more realistic, by claiming it took 40 years to build, and opened in 1858.

The question is, was this marvellous structure completed in 1858? Or was it merely inherited in 1858? If so, who were the original builders, and where did the builders go?

Things get a little puzzling however, in the form of a lithography of architect, Auguste de Montferrand's drawing from 1710, of the first St. Isaac's Church.

Here we see a massive single storey building, complete with bell tower, domes, antennae, and a number of slender, towering spires in the background. In the foreground, the odd horse or two and several human figures stroll the muddy street. Then lo and behold, we can clearly see a ship's anchor, buried half in, and half out of the mud.

Paintings and drawings prove nothing of course. But if a picture paints a thousand words, then what is the artist trying to say?

According to 'Stolen History', "apparently there is this theory in Russia, that Peter the Great was **not** the founder of Saint Petersburg. He did not build the city, he dug it out."

Whether true or not, I wouldn't know, but like many countries across the realm, there is plenty of visual evidence in Eastern Europe, for buildings with windows entirely below, or partially buried below ground level.

We are told the Saint Mary's Basilica in Kraków, Poland, was completed in 1347, with additions made in the first half of the fifteenth century. Exterior photographs taken of the lower level, provide undeniable evidence that the original ground level of the main building, is now a minimum of 6-8 feet below the current ground level. Did the Basilica sink 6 feet into the ground under its own weight? Or did something occur to deposit an additional 6 feet of earth upon the original ground level?

Again, the perfect copper layering and the architectural symmetry of the building's grand interior, which we thought was art, was not just art, but visual old world technology meticulously carved into the stonework.

Wikipedia inform us that during the eighteenth century, all 26 altars, equipment, furniture, benches and paintings were *replaced* and the walls were decorated with polychrome.

Whilst there's no way of knowing for certain, I strongly suspect that the interior altars, furniture, and paintings etc. were *not* replaced, but *added* for cosmetic and religious purposes. For over the years 1887–1891, we're told the building gained a new design, murals were painted and stained glass was *added* to the presbytery. Prior to the nineteenth century there is no mention of stained glass.

A Hidden Secret?

In his classic 1831 novel, *'The Hunchback of Notre-Dame'*, Victor Hugo revealed that classical architecture which arose during the Renaissance of the 1400s and reigned until the beginning of the nineteenth century, had an agenda which was dead set on replacing, and in turn destroying the medieval architecture of the Middle Ages.

In 1946, and having left the written manuscript of *'Le Mystère des Cathédrales'* with his only student, Eugène Canseliet, the enigmatic French alchemist and author Fulcanelli, mysteriously disappeared after the liberation of Paris, never to be seen again. Fulcanelli's book which was published after his disappearance in 1946, informs us that the great cathedrals "once held a mystery".

In one of his videos, Ewaranon remarks;

"Between them, Fulcanelli and Victor Hugo, suggest the cathedrals once held a *secret* which a force in this world did not want us to know about."

Could there be an element of truth in this? Did the cathedrals once hold a mystery, a secret? For why would the builders go to such extreme lengths to create these magnificent structures unless there was a grander purpose?

Where Victor Hugo talks about the people of his time, defacing or destroying many of the grand old buildings, please bear in mind they also had the technology, to add facades and stone cladding to the existing structures and even to build imitations.

The Victorian restoration period directly affected around 80% of the ecclesiastical structures in England, especially the medieval ones. From the addition of stone cladding and facades via restoration, to demolition and then rebuilding. It was during this time period that the church interiors were redecorated, standardized and in many cases, completely rewritten.

If indeed, an entire chunk of British and American history has been deliberately hidden, the process of doing so, most likely occurred during this same period of time.

Free Energy

The iconic 'Blue Marble' we're all familiar with, is nothing more than a figment of the imagination, conjured up primarily by NASA, and promoted by the scientific community at large.

Contrary to what we have all been taught since childhood, the Earth we dwell upon, is not some random, spinning ball of rock careering around the central Sun, whilst spiralling on a never-ending journey through the darkest regions of outer space.

The Earth we dwell upon is far, far, far more magnificent than that, yet in ways that are as simple as they are profound.

Simply put, the Earth exists ***not*** as a moving planet within the Firmament above. Earth is not a planet, but a circular and stationary realm which is relatively flat, and exists directly beneath the Firmament. The Magnetic North Pole, which is located at the centre of the circular, stationary and relatively flat Earth, is precisely aligned with Polaris, otherwise known as the North Star, which is situated high in the Firmament above.

Like a Majestic Celestial Timepiece, the heavenly bodies in the Firmament above, are in a continual state of transit as they slowly revolve around Polaris above and the circle of the Earth below.

According to ancient and medieval science, Aether, also known as the fifth element or quintessence, is the material that fills the region of the heavens beyond the terrestrial realm. Aether was assumed to be weightless, transparent, frictionless, undetectable chemically or physically, and literally permeating all matter and space. The concept of aether has been used in several theories to explain certain natural phenomena, such as the ability of light to travel.

Modern-day pseudoscience has rejected the existence of Aether by calling it Dark Energy and Dark Matter,which according to sources such as Wikipedia;

is a hypothetical form of matter, which is thought to account for approximately 85% of the matter in the universe.

Albert Einstein published his two theories of relativity in 1905 and 1916. With the general theory of relativity, the Aether was finally abolished in physics. Yet in retrospect, even Einstein himself was uncomfortable with this, and later tried to clarify that his theories would not work at all without the aether.

But the damage was done.

Stanford University Professor of Physics, Robert B. Laughlin, wrote:

> It is ironic that Einstein's most creative work, the general theory of relativity, should boil down to conceptualizing space as a medium when his original premise [in Special Relativity] was that no such medium existed.

Gamma, X-ray, ultraviolet light and visible light from the Sun (electric current) forms in contact with Earth's magnetic field forming an infinite, recharging energy source. The Magnetosphere (which is not a sphere) is defined as the region of space above the Earth's Ionosphere (which is not a sphere) in which charged-particle motion is dominated by the geomagnetic field. Without which there would be no life on Earth.

The existence of Ley Lines on earth was promoted by the English antiquarian Alfred Watkins in the 1920's, which by and large has been ridiculed by main stream Academia, as being nothing more than ancient esoteric tradition.

Are the lines real?

Yes, because the Earth constantly creates electric currents called Telluric earth currents, which criss-cross the earth's entire surface in alignment with electromagnetic lines.

Evidently, the Earth and Ionosphere have a charge differential which can be discharged wirelessly anywhere on, above or inside the Earth by manipulating and bouncing the energy off the Ionosphere. For there is no energy in matter, other than what is conferred to it by virtue of its existence within The Aetheric field.

This concept is not some type of wild theory or fantasy, for it was proven and demonstrated by Nikola Tesla, who transmitted Free Energy across the Earth wirelessly. Hence wireless itself is evidence of The Aetheric field.

One such demonstration was levelling an estimated 80 million trees over an area of 830 square miles of the Tunguska Forest in Siberia on 30 June, 1908.

Although no impact crater or telltale fragments of rock have ever been found, the cover story for this event, was a rogue meteor which entered Earth's atmosphere and exploded in mid-air at an altitude of 3 to 6 miles.

Returning to the Tartarians, it's thought by many that this advanced people or civilization not only built huge brick and stone structures to extract and store the energy harnessed from the ionosphere, but crafted them with such finesse and beauty, perhaps as a celebration of gratitude for their acquired understanding and skill.

Effectively, the buildings they constructed were both functional and crafted as a homage to that function. For these magnificent brick and stone buildings, topped with long metal spikes or antennae, were intentionally constructed to channel energy from the Aether above, for the sole purpose of creating free, powerful and clean wireless electromagnetic energy.

Simply put, these long conducting rods functioned like the Anode and Cathode on a battery where the energy is converted into long wavelengths (ELF) which bounce off the Ionosphere back to Earth.

The common use of antiferromagnetic dielectric metals for the antennae was deliberate, in order to illicit and excite various electromagnetic effects, in much the same way as capacitors are employed, using dielectric materials in modern electronics.

And they had access to this technology during the time that official history calls the middle age aka the Dark Age.

Although ferrous objects will respond more dramatically to direct magnetic fields, *all* objects are effected by the mere existence of the Aetheric field, regardless of their magnetic properties.

Let me be honest here, for my knowledge of electromagnetism and indeed, physics in general, is about as basic as it gets. So here is the briefest and simplest explanation I could find, courtesy of *'Science Direct'*. Please note however, that I have taken the liberty of substituting the word "generator" for "ionosphere".

I have done so, not to be deceptive, but because the theory in question, proposes that just like a generator, the ionosphere itself, is the source of the energy.

> Electromagnetic energy is transmitted from the *ionosphere* to antennas or other radiating systems in which oscillating currents are set up over a wide band of frequencies corresponding to the frequencies of the *ionosphere*. These in turn induce similar currents in surrounding bodies and regions of matter.

The following is derived from Peter John Ladetto's Analysis on Aether.

Modern science, (Physics in particular), has trapped itself inside its own fantasy-land of objects, both large and small, which do not behave as scientists describe, or simply, do not exist at all. It is unnecessary to unify that which is already One Energy, which is exactly what the concept of Aether points to. Aetheric energy is a metaphysical fluid of tangible and homogeneously isotropic pressure. Electricity, Gravity, Magnetism, and Dielectricity are not separate forces. Rather, these are all specific modalities of a Unified Field under various forms of stress and strain.

In other words, the Aetheric field is not merely a magnetic field. Rather, it exists as the interplay between both magnetic and dielectric (non-magnetic) potentialities, acting as a singular unified substrate, or Aetheric perturbation modality, for all matter, whether ferrous (magnetic) or not. And any disturbance (perturbation) of the Aether will translate as mechanical motion.

Writes researcher and prolific author, Gregory Garrett;

Magnetic induction is the production of an electromotive force across an electrical conductor in a changing magnetic field. Hence, Light, Magnetism, and Sound are all Aetheric field perturbation dependent in their transmission, and not the result of particles or waves in motion.

Whilst I don't profess to completely understand the concept of Aether and Electromagnetism, by any stretch of the imagination, this is not some 'New Age' idea. It is grounded in electromagnetic field systems and vibrational frequencies.

Even we, as bio-electric beings, are directly affected by the changes in the environment's electromagnetic field. Our bodies are formed by the same ions from the aether and are 70 % water.

Our personal bio-electromagnetic field is connected to the Earth, and we are held in equilibrium with the Earth's electromagnetic field through sympathetic resonance.

Magnetism and electricity are inextricable. Water is the driving life force of all carbon-based life forms on earth and earth is governed by electromagnetism, frequency and vibration. Essentially, the hidden force of electro-magnetism maintains all life on Earth.

Nikola Tesla understood the concept of free energy harnessed from the heavens above, and demonstrated how it could be transmitted wirelessly to any location here on earth below.

He also published the plans for extracting limitless energy from the

Sun and sequestering unlimited nitrogen from the Atmosphere for world-wide farming in 1900.

He was murdered because of this knowledge in his hotel room in New York, on 7 January, 1943. All of Tesla's inventions, prototypes, blueprints and work documents were seized by the U.S. Government authorities.

I suspect there were two agendas in play at the time. For it is extremely likely that the controllers used Tesla, by effectively allowing him to experiment with old world technology for a limited period of time. After his death, it gave the controllers an opportunity to ridicule and debunk Tesla's ideas and inventions, and shelve this superior technology for all time.

For in the meanwhile, Donald Trump's uncle John G. Trump, an MIT research scientist, conceptually weaponized Nikola Tesla's technology patents for the US Army before handing the stolen technology over to Joseph Stalin at the end of WWII.

As with any form of technology, the gathering of free energy can be used for both good and evil purposes. The love of money is the root of all evil *(1 Timothy 6:10)* and the energy which was formerly free and used for good, would now be monetized, and used in part, for great evil.

The United States and the Soviet Union began secret cooperation on world weather-engineering in 1971, and now there are dozens of International Geo-engineering and Weather Modification programs dating back to that time.

The discovery of this unlimited energy source which exists only in the firmament of the heavens above, has gone largely unnoticed because of the great secrecy with which it has been held by all who know of it. Incomprehensible injustice has been perpetrated to develop the ultimate weapon system.

Modern-day Electromagnetic Weaponry is invisible, silent, requires no medium, has unlimited firepower, at low cost once the hardware and methods are established, and travels at the speed of light.

Satanists and their minions in Governments invest in Weather Derivatives and create Earthquakes and Weather Modification aka Geo-Engineering.

The Satanists who control the electro-magnetic field today, are using it to manipulate the world's weather systems, and artificially create wildfires, hurricanes and earthquakes etc. in order to promote the global warming scam, to drastically reduce world population and to destroy the Earth.

At least eight individual countries have HAARP (High Frequency Active Auroral Research Project) style facilities; most are in places where the radiation belts guide enormous amounts of solar energy to the polar regions of the earth. Vostok in Antarctica is one such ELF (Extremely Low Facility), and the Soviet Era 'Wood Pecker Grid' in Russia is another.

Since the Korean War, dozens of weather modification experiments such as 'Storm Fury' and 'Sky Fox' have been carried out. In fact, many nations of the world have been altering the weather for at least 50 years, and it's done by heating water just like we do in a microwave oven. Heat the atmosphere by vibrating the Ionosphere and one has a very effective weapon for bringing down satellites and intercontinental ballistic missiles as well.

If you believe the official narrative surrounding the 2010 Deepwater Horizon incident and the 2011 Fukushima nuclear disaster, you are very much mistaken. Both incidents were intentionally created by the controllers, with the use of scalar technology.

It was no coincidence Deep Water Horizon was set ablaze on Weed Day and scuttled on Earth Day, nor has the oil and methane release stopped.

Fukushima was designed to fail by the Rockefeller Foundation, and the site was chosen and intentionally flooded because it is the site where the atmospheric Jet Stream originates, and the site where three major Pacific Ocean currents collide. Our oceans are being poisoned, for Fukushima radiation, which incidentally has never stopped, has been called "the gift which keeps on giving".

They are even using Magnetogenetics, a biological technique that involves the use of magnetic fields to remotely control human brain cell activity from a distance.

These are not a conspiracy theories, but are conspiracy facts, which are recorded in the public domain.

Sound and Water

The second verse in the Bible, informs us that prior to the First Day of the 6 day Restoration, all was in total darkness, there was water literally everywhere, and the barren and lifeless Earth was completely submerged beneath the face of the Deep, which according to Job was frozen. *(Job 38:30)*.

These were the waters of Death, the aftermath of the cataclysmic flood that wiped out the aeon or world that existed back in the heavens of old, leaving the earth of old standing both in and out of the water. *(2 Peter 3:4-7.)*

God separated the waters below from the waters above with the expanse of the firmament which contains the celestial bodies. He used Magnetite in the mantle beneath Earth's crust to create a magnetic field using the Sun's electric current which diverts deadly Gamma rays, X-rays, and U-V radiation from reaching the Earth.

Genesis 1:2 tells us that " the Spirit of God moved upon the face of the waters."

Although we're given no details, I think it safe to assume that from the moment God spoke Light into the darkness, the Sound of His Voice energized the waters, transforming them into Waters of life, or Living Waters.

For whilst Adam's physical body was formed from the dust of the ground, every other living creature, including birds and water fowl, sprang into being from the waters. Even the Earth itself arose from the watery depths in response to the spoken command of God.

Genesis 1:9-10. And God said, Let the **waters** under the heaven be gathered together unto one place, and let the dry land **appear**: And God called the dry land Earth.

Genesis 1:20-21. And God said, Let the **waters** bring forth abundantly the moving creature that hath life, and fowl *that* may fly above the earth in the open firmament of heaven. And God created great whales, and every living creature that moveth, **which the waters brought forth abundantly**, after their kind, and **every winged fowl** after his kind: and God saw that *it was* good.

Although the deeper mysteries of the creation are known only to the Word who was with God and who was God in the beginning, maybe the written Word, the Scriptures themselves, invite us to ask the question;

Did the majestic Voice of God, influence the entire molecular structure of the water, effectively energizing it by way of sound, frequency and vibration?

I strongly suspect so, yes.

Electrical genius, Nikola Tesla once said;

"If you want to find the secrets of the universe, think in terms of energy, frequency and vibration."

The extraordinary life-work of the Japanese scientist, Dr. Masaru Emoto, demonstrated how the spoken words and thoughts of humans, especially when verbalized in prayer, impacts the physical realm.

For over 20 years until he passed away in 2014, he studied the scientific evidence of how the molecular structure in water transforms when it is exposed to words, thoughts, sounds and intentions. He did this through Magnetic Resonance Analysis technology and high-speed photography.

In his 2004 New York Times Bestseller book, *"The Hidden Messages in Water"*, Dr. Emoto demonstrates how water exposed to benevolent and compassionate human words and intention, results in aesthetically pleasing physical molecular formations in the water.

On the other hand, water that is exposed to fearful and discordant human intentions results in disconnected, disfigured and noticeably unpleasant physical molecular formations.

His research also showed how polluted and toxic water, when exposed to prayer and benevolent intention, can be altered and restored to beautifully formed, geometric crystal-like patterns found in clean, healthy water.

Experiments show this truly remarkable change in the molecular structure of water, can also be produced by the vibrational sound frequency of classical, symphony music for example, especially when compared to the jarring vibrational sound frequency of heavy metal. One creates intricate molecular patterns of harmony and splendour, whilst the other produces gross and distorted patterns of discordance.

Cymatics

Cymatics is described as the study of wave phenomena, especially sound, and their visual representations.

The study of Cymatics reveals that sound vibrations excite matter into geometric forms which coincide with the unique mathematical relationship which is called the Golden Ratio, also known as the Golden Mean, or Divine Proportion.

Experiments show that everything oscillates, vibrates, and undulates in nature, which orchestrates geometries found throughout the natural world.

Truly amazing resonance experiments can be seen on YouTube, which reveal a fabric of reality that has always been present, but one that most of us never knew existed.

Salt, for example, when poured onto a simple metal plate, and using a tone generator causing the plate to vibrate. As the pitch of the tone increases, the grains of salt flow outward from the centre of the plate, forming incredible, unique and beautiful geometric patterns, which much like a snowflake, become increasingly more complex.

Back in the eighteenth century, the German poet and scientist, Johann Wolfgang von Goethe, stated;

"*Music* is *liquid architecture* and *Architecture* is *frozen music*".

I'm sure most of us have experienced the profound, and almost tangible silence felt within an empty church building, at some point in our life. This is not the presence of God, as some might assume. For God does not dwell "in temples made with hands". *(Acts 17:24.)* The silence has more to do with resonance and acoustics.

In 1973, Tanya Harris, who describes herself as a multidisciplinary artist, set out to investigate this concept further. To do so, she recorded the resonant frequency of four individual late 17th to early 18th century churches, each we're told, designed in the Baroque style, by English architect, Nicholas Hawksmoor.

Harris recorded the actual silence of each church and played this recording back into the church while re-recording, and repeated this process until the resonant frequencies of the church became audible.

Furthermore, by placing a small bowl of water in a loudspeaker, and noting the precise vibrational pattern form on the water's surface, she discovered the hidden geometry of these resonant frequencies.

The richness of sound influenced the entire molecular structure of the water. Furthermore, in many cases these sound-induced vibrational patterns, mirror the pattern of the rose windows found in the church building itself. Hence translating sound recorded from the architecture of an empty stone building, into astounding liquid architecture.

Others have used the same technique to study the patterns which form when bells resound within these structures. Again, the patterns formed within the water are almost identical to those carved into the stonework of rose windows. Consider the incredible craftsmanship of the huge rose window at Strasbourg Cathedral for example.

It is no coincidence, that the cymatic patterns which are formed in water by the richness and depth of a reverberating bell, and the precise geometry of rose windows resemble each other so closely. Nor that the entire ceilings of the great cathedrals also mirror this same cymatic geometry.

Distinctively crafted as though an architecture within an architecture the three-dimensional geometry of the fan vaulted ceilings are of spectacular quality. A fan vault as seen at Bath Abbey, is described as a form of vault used in the Gothic style, in which the masonry ribs are all of the same curve and spaced equidistantly, in a manner resembling a fan.

Why would a supposedly underdeveloped people spend so much time, money and effort into crafting such perfect and symmetrical ornamentation? Especially if it had no function and was purely aesthetic. Could they be crafted by hand today, and at such height?

When closely examining the interior of these cathedral ceilings, arches and domes, one can see they rely heavily on symmetrical ornamentation. This was achieved by the indentations or cavities, meticulously carved into the masonry.

The floral and fractal designs diligently carved with such finesse, into the rectangular niches and panels, along with the intricate three dimensional stone ribbing seen on the underside of the interior ceilings, arches and domes, were never intended for decorative or structural purposes.

These imposing wonders of stone geometry were designed as an integral and functional part of something much larger. A massive generator of power.

Iron rods were used right from the initial construction phase, and ran throughout the stone infrastructure, some of which can still be seen today in sections of the broken masonry and shattered stone columns. These metal bars were complimented with the distinctive blue copper or gold roofed domes and arches, that can be seen everywhere. It's also been estimated by some experts, that these metallic domed structures were designed to last for at least one thousand years, before the need for any major repair.

Furthermore, according to some researchers, the limestone or granite used for construction was mixed with silicon crystals or quartz, which has great electrical potential. As with everything else in the old world these grand buildings were both functional and crafted in homage to that function.

It's now believed by many, including myself, that the harnessing and storage of free energy from the aether was achieved by using huge energy gathering stone buildings with large copper coils and other old world technology fitted on rooftops and within the rotundas and domes.

Complete with metal poles, situated atop strategically placed spires, cupolas and towers, which acted as electrical antennas, which in turn harnessed the power of the aether.

That harnessed free energy was then focused into large purpose-built domes, each designed with vaulted and high fluted ceilings and intricately sculpted rose windows and interiors, which acted as magnetrons and resonators.

There is a striking similarity between the perfect three-dimensional, symmetrical ornamentation of a rose window carved from stone, and the pattern seen on a magnetron, of the type found in microwave ovens etc. Is this merely coincidence?

According to Wikipedia, a "magnetron is an electronic valve that works as an oscillator in the microwave range of the electromagnetic spectrum."

Magnetrons can be seen everywhere in these structures, beautifully crafted into stone walls, arched windows, doorways and vaulted ceilings, with such expertise, and virtually impossible to replicate today.

The precise floral designs intricately carved into the recessed stonework, acted as acoustic resonators, continually vibrating energy particles into electro-magnetic energy of specific frequencies. Meticulously carved circular stone rose windows, were never designed to hold glass; but acted as cavity magnetrons to generate energy.

The controllers who **inherited** these wonderful buildings, merely added stained glass at a later date, to shut off the magnetron's function. In most cases they redesignated the building as a religious place of worship.

None can be certain of course, but it's believed that magnetrons and resonators would have to work in conjunction with a central engine, which was probably similar to a nuclear reactor.

These engines and reactors were usually, but not always, located in octagonal structures found on the ground floor, or in close proximity to the main building.

The controllers have since systematically removed all traces of the physical apparatus, but often left the empty shell where the engine used to reside. These empty shells are usually octagonal, and can be seen in government buildings and cathedrals etc. worldwide.

Some have since been covered over or left barren, but many have been repurposed as gazebos, rotundas, baptistry's and bandstands etc.

Red brick and concrete are excellent conductors of electricity, and red brickwork was very often used in these old world structures. Interestingly, scientists have recently discovered that red brick made from iron oxide is capable of storing electrical charges as a form of solid state battery.

The larger concrete and red brick buildings, which acted as huge energy storage batteries, were designated and recognizable by their white stripes. Such as the massive 689 feet long St. Pancras Railway Station in London, and many other famous structures across the realm. Other energy storage buildings were constructed with brown and white, or blue and white, stripes.

Metallic coils can still be seen at the top of many old world buildings across the Earth, and it is believed that the abundance of small rotundas and cupolas situated atop many of these buildings, and which now stand empty, have had their original apparatus removed. This would have included the use of mercury, a vital factor in harnessing free electromagnetic energy.

Amazing demonstrations can be seen on YouTube which show the outcome of passing a flow of electricity through a bowl of mercury which contains a magnet. Deflected by the magnet, the electrons cause the mercury to rotate creating a vortex. Even today it is still common practice for lighthouses with large Fresnel lenses to use mercury baths as a low-friction, rotation mechanism.

It would also explain the worldwide abundance of the antennae designed in the shape of the mercury symbol. It's critical to understand that a lot of the icons and symbols that adorn these antennae were never meant to represent different religions in the old world.

They signified something else entirely, and were usually made from copper and gold, both being excellent conductors of electricity. Antennae were never religious symbols but designed to transmit energy to other antennas.

Whilst some might question the symbolic design of some of the antennae, it is very likely that the controllers have since associated these symbols with other, darker things that were not their original meaning.

The towers, the spires, the domes, the antennae, the colonnades and the arches we see everywhere across the realm, were once essential components of the electromagnetic infrastructure. Each designed to mirror and enhance the flow of electromagnetic energy.

This is why every panoramic view looking out across the roof tops of any major city worldwide, you will see scores of minarets, stone towers, steeples and spires, spiked antennae, metal conductor orbs and copper or gold domed resonators. They are literally everywhere.

These skilfully crafted, energy gathering red brick, concrete and stone structures, which once operated as generators, batteries and capacitors, have been repurposed, and are now understood as being government buildings, palaces, castles, mosques, cathedrals and churches, of which there are hundreds of thousands across the entire realm.

As of December 2018, there were 3,391 Cathedral-status buildings around the world, predominantly in countries with a significant Roman Catholic population.

These strategically located buildings were never constructed to be government buildings, palaces for the rich and famous or even places of worship. They were meticulously designed and erected for the overall benefit of the world's population at the time.

Most were complex buildings, each beautifully constructed complete with towers designed to house huge resonating bells, and in many cases with magnificent pipe organs situated on the lower level. The Pipe Organ being the King of sound, the richest and loudest traditional instrument in the world.

Like the glorious structures they reside in, these superior and massive instruments of sound, are marvels of craftsmanship, both of elegance and majesty.

More than that, experiments have shown that the vibrational frequencies of the richness of sound produced by the pipe organ can have a positive therapeutic effect on the human body.

Energized Water

It is believed that the principle method used for the distribution of therapeutic energy, was achieved through energizing water with the use of acoustics, vibrational frequency and sympathetic resonance. Hence why so many of these remarkable old buildings were surrounded by moats, and built in the vicinity of lakes, rivers or canals.

While history records the Volga-Don Canal was built in the 1950's its construction actually began back in the sixteenth century. The world's entire major canal and aqueduct system was inherited from the original builders.

Running through rivers and reservoirs, the Volga-Don Canal (if the Mediterranean is counted) connects the Caspian Sea with the world's oceans, via the Sea of Azov and the Black Sea. The Suez Canal connects the North Atlantic and northern Indian oceans via the Mediterranean Sea and the Red Sea. *(Credit:Lost History of Flat Earth.)*

In turn, the Panama Canal connects the Atlantic Ocean with the Pacific Ocean, and the Corinth Canal connects the Ionian Sea with the Aegean Sea, thus creating a vast worldwide network of interconnected waterways.

Whoever designed them, understood that water is the key to

unlocking the full potential of free electro-magnetic energy.

It's also believed that the direct current (DC) system was used at the time, rather than the alternating current (AC) system which is generally used today. Either way, the words "current" and "flow" have been retained and applied to electricity.

In this ingenious manner the entire region, most likely even the entire Earth, effectively became a giant circuit board powered by the Aether. A worldwide free energy electro-magnetic grid system.

Star Stations

Star cities, star forts or star stations, some of which were isolated, whilst others comprised of entire cities, were not constructed for military or fortification purposes, as we are led to believe. Each star station was perfectly and geometrically designed to be an integral working part of this world-wide, interconnected energy grid.

In a number of instances, these star forts have even retained the name "batteries", although most are now invariably used as military garrisons.

Star stations found in the UK include, Berwick-upon-Tweed, Brighton, Dover, Falmouth, Fareham, Felixstowe, Gosport, London, Inverness, Plymouth and Portsmouth. There are many more.

City-status star stations scattered right across Europe include, Amsterdam, Alessandria, Bayonne, Berlin, Bethune, Breda, Brielle, Bourtange, Casal, Cologne, Copenhagen, Dresden, Hamburg, Heusden, Lisle, Nicosia, Terezín, Turin, Vienna and Willemstad.

Furthermore, star stations can be found throughout the USA, and indeed, are scattered across the entire earth. Each individual star station has the same common denominator; for all once had an intricate waterway system, and all were once surrounded by water.

Many have since been drained or destroyed by the controllers of history, to hide the evidence of this former electromagnetic water-world of oscillating frequencies of sound, and vibration.

In the same manner as the perfectly carved magnetrons and resonators found in the old world buildings, the precise symmetrical arrangement and sharp angles of the star stations, would cause the molecules and ions in the flowing water to perpetually vibrate.

The stunning geometric precision and perfect symmetry of the star stations, is believed to have enhanced the generators and batteries, and aetherised the water's entire molecular structure, hence creating energized or pure 'Living Water'.

Many of these former energy gathering structures have huge underground reservoirs, cavities or cisterns for storing water, some of which have been drained and some kept intact. Most of the so-called Victorian underground water cisterns and reservoirs, still stretch for miles beneath our cities.

In a number of cases, the exterior water storage cisterns have been redesignated as Roman Baths, which is why Bath Cathedral in England is located right next to the Roman baths.

In other parts of the world especially the Indian subcontinent, water was often stored in Stepwells, which is why they were constructed with such precise and complex geometric patterns. Stepwells usually consist of two parts: a vertical shaft from which water is drawn, and surrounding the shaft, the inclined and precision built, underground passageways, chambers and steps which provide access to the well.

Perhaps the most classic example is the Rani Ki Vav Stepwell, located on the banks of the Saraswati river in India. The well remained buried in silt until the 1980's, when it was allegedly rediscovered and restored.

At 33 feet in diameter and 98 feet deep this architectural wonder in beauty of detail and proportions, is divided into seven levels of stairs which lead down to a deep circular well. A stepped corridor is compartmentalized at regular intervals with pillared, multi-storey pavilions and hundreds of sculptural panels. *(Credit:Wikipedia.)*

It's believed the vibrational frequency of the sound of the water as it tumbled down from level to level, played a pivotal role in the energizing process.

Water was stored and manipulated for a variety of reasons in reservoirs, underground cisterns, water towers, pumping stations and other structures, in ways more futuristic than perhaps we can even begin to imagine. For the electromagnetic water grid was not just an energized version of what we are all familiar with, but in all likelihood had many uses and applications way beyond our comprehension.

The entire medieval water course grid was destabilized and deactivated by the controllers somewhere between the 17th and 19th centuries. Spring water has to go somewhere, and one way they achieved this here in the UK it would seem, was by redirecting the water through hundreds of underground culverts and rivers. Wikipedia has nearly 4 pages listing subterranean rivers in the UK. London for example, has a total of twenty one underground rivers and streams.

Maybe this all sounds far too mystical for some. Even too far fetched. Yet it would almost seem that in the not too distant past, a people inhabited the Earth, who possessed an understanding, maybe even a divine knowledge, of the true nature and potential of God's Miraculous Creation.

At what point in time, those who constructed this impossible system, seemingly disappeared, along with their technology is unknown. Yet it appears that the importance and understanding of the properties of acoustic resonance became a faded memory, a shadow of the past.

Considered to be folklore, there are an abundance of old tales here in the UK, of church bells being destroyed, buried, and thrown into lakes, rivers or oceans. One such tale is centred around the coastal village of Bosham, West Sussex, not too far from my home town.

The story tells of a crew of pirates who carried off the tenor bell of the local monastery. Due to its size and weight, the bell sank through both the deck and the hold of the vessel to the bottom of a great hole in Bosham channel, known to this day as the "Bell Hole".

Writes historian, Mark Antony Lower, in *"A Compendious History of Sussex: Topographical, Archœological & Anecdotical" (1870 p.67)*

> It is still the belief of the good folk of Bosham that though the bell is deep down in the water, it has not lost its power of resonance, and that whenever a sturdy peal is rung out from the church tower, the lost tenor chimes in with her sister bells, and those standing at the brink of the "Bell Hole " can distinctly hear the whole octave peal.

Similar tales can be found throughout the UK. Why are there so many stories of church bells being destroyed? Resentment and anger maybe, because their resonance no longer energized the water?

Or could it be because they emanated a particular vibration, which due to its acoustic resonance, now had a negative effect on the human body?

Maybe there's an alternative reason for the destruction of so many bells, but I can't think of one right at the moment.

Many have since explored the powerful connection between sound and water, and scientists have found that ultrasonic water can treat the most resistant of infections and heal wounds. As too can vibrational frequencies.

Big Pharma

Founded in 1863 by John D. Rockefeller and industrialist Henry Flagle, 'The Standard Oil Company' was incorporated in 1870. By the turn of the 20th century, Rockefeller controlled 90% of all oil refineries in the US through the Standard Oil company, which was later broken up to become Chevron, Exxon and Mobil etc.

On 14 May, 1913, John D. Rockefeller and John D. Rockefeller Jr. established The Rockefeller Foundation in New York.

In the early 1900's, scientists discovered "petrochemicals" and the ability to create all kinds of chemicals from oil. The best thing about petrochemicals was that everything produced could now be patented and sold for huge profits.

As reported in April, 2019 by 'World Affairs';

"This was a wonderful opportunity for Rockefeller, who saw the ability to monopolize the oil, chemical and the medical industries all at one and the same time".

There was one major problem; for natural or herbal medicines were still very popular in America at the time. An estimated 50% of all doctors and medical establishments were practising holistic or natural medicines.

When the truth slowly began to emerge that a number of petroleum based medicines were actually causing cancer, the Rockefeller Foundation suppressed that information and largely financed 'The American Cancer Society', which was also founded in 1913.

Along with his sphere of influence and control over the education system, the stage was set. Any mention of the natural health benefits gained from herbs and plants etc. was erased from most medical text books, and the robber baron John D. Rockefeller became duly recognized as the founder of the Pharmaceutical Industry. Today, no industry has more power over the lives of humanity than Big Pharma.

Remedies that had been used for thousand of years were now labelled as Alternative Medicine, whilst modern drugs (many of which are highly addictive) were declared to be the new Gold

Standard.

Doctors and professors who objected to Rockefeller's plan for monopolisation, were discredited and marginalized by the media, and in many cases removed from the American Medical Association or had their licenses revoked. Any who dared to speak out were arrested and jailed for practising quackery.

In 1934, American inventor, Royal Raymond Rife, successfully treated 16 out of 16 terminally ill patients with various cancers in less than 70 days, using his hand built vibrational frequency device. He knew that everything vibrates at its own natural frequency, and believed that if he could discover the frequency of disease-causing microorganisms, he could destroy them with the same vibrational frequency.

Although he came to collaborate with other inventors, scientists and doctors, and his findings were published in a number of newspapers and scientific journals, for obvious financial reasons, his work was quickly suppressed, and he was declared a fraud.

Cancer treatment is a highly lucrative business, which is protected at any cost it would seem. Hence some promoters of Rife's work have since been convicted of health fraud and even sent to prison.

One can only conclude that there are powerful forces in our world that don't want us to go back into a state of abundance and health.

Yet it appears that a collective memory of the old world system of energized water remained, at least for a generation or so.

Old stone wells can still be found in some English towns and villages with *"A Well of Living Water"* carved into the stonework, and one small village has a dried up drinking fountain, dated 1876, bearing the inscription;

"The Lord's Gift".

Artificial Landscape

Vast and sprawling parklands as part of our national heritage are found in abundance, along with stately homes in their hundreds, right across the UK. But the surrounding countryside, including the rivers and lakes, are *not* what they seem, for they are *not* normal or natural, they are artificial.

In a more recent video, gifted researcher, Ewaranon, brings to our attention, that during the eighteenth century, unfathomable quantities of earth were shifted to create hills, redesign waterways, and to cover the landscape of England, and in many cases, to bury the remains of the old world structures and the monasteries that existed before it. Constructing classical-style architecture in their stead.

We are told, that Lancelot, aka Capability Brown, was responsible for redesigning the natural landscape and surroundings of more than 170 stately homes and mansions throughout England.

Prior to this, the design of the fields, the tiered terraces and gardens, the canals and the waterways across virtually the entire land, were based on precise geometrical formations.

Write David Brown & Tom Williamson in *'Lancelot Brown and the Capability Men', 2016, p.78*;

> removed avenues, parterres, terraces, basins and canals-everything partaking of the old art and geometry from the environs of great houses. In their place, they laid out what we now describe as "landscape parks" , informal and "natural" in character, eschewing straight lines and formal geometry.

Of the vast Longleat estate the authors describe how;

> terraces were to be levelled, land drained and walls removed, various basins and canals filled in or de-formalised, and trees and shrubs planted, and gravel walks laid out [....] A ha-ha was to be constructed and modifications made to the existing "serpentine water", so that its "sharp turns" were removed.*(p.75.)*

> What is so striking about these endeavours is that, until we are told that this great effort has been made, we would often not know it. *(p.114.)*

Since the early part of the seventeenth century, the Parliament of Great Britain, had passed a large number of Enclosure Acts, meaning the land surrounding these sites, no longer belonged to the common people. Their rights of access were removed, and fields were enclosed by hedges, walls and fences.

The powers granted in the Inclosure Act of 1773, were often abused by landowners, and by 1914, over 5,200 individual enclosure acts were passed, affecting 6,800,000 acres" or "one-fifth of the total area of England and Wales."

In many cases this abuse, and infringement upon the common people destroyed entire communities leaving many families with little choice than to relocate and seek work elsewhere.

But this nation-wide operation credited to Brown, was not the work of one man, but of hundreds, if not thousands of men. Brown was part of an intricate network of patrons, contractors, subcontractors, and suppliers, and there is some tantalising evidence to indicate that, under the direction of the former military engineer, John Wooton, the military, hence the English government, were in control of the whole earth moving operation. Capability Brown, the great 'Earth Mover', is just the cover story for an agenda we are not privy to, for it is not recorded in the official record.

It is truly astonishing how so much time, money and effort was put into changing everything, including the historical narrative. For we have no real way of knowing what the former medieval landscape may actually have looked like. Nor how many medieval, old-world structures may have been demolished and buried by the massive and mind-boggling amounts of earth that were shifted during the complete redesigning, of the natural landscape of vast areas of England.

It would be impossible to estimate the unfathomable tonnage of earth that was shifted by the earth movers of the eighteenth century. as they redesigned and changed vast swathes of the national landscape. Effectively hiding centuries of British history, and the suppression of information, equal in scale to that of medieval book-burning.

I'm not sure about the other nations of the world, but earth moving operations were also taking place in America, and on a scale that literally goes off the charts.

Something is wrong with the official narrative, and it is highly disturbing. For at the end of the day, what is earth if it is not soil? And what is soil if it is not dirt? And what is dirt, if it is not MUD?

What Happened?

Some say an apocalyptic mud flood partially buried many of the old world buildings, whilst others suggest an unknown type of plasma weaponry was used to destroy the more obvious signs of this former Tartarian infrastructure. Certainly city fires and wars have since played a major role in the destruction of the old world architecture.

As for myself, personally I find it very hard, impossible in fact, to believe that any civilization, Tartarian or otherwise, which has descended over the generations, from one of the three sons of Noah, has had access to such a form of technology.

Nevertheless, after having spent countless hours considering the evidence presented by others, as well as doing my own research, I've slowly come to the same shared conclusion.

An undefined period of world history has been purposefully hidden from the official public record. And believe me, for much like the true design of the Earth, when one starts to see such things, they cannot be 'unseen'.

It was during this "missing" period of time when these huge majestic buildings were constructed, and in such an impossible manner that for numerous reasons, cannot be replicated today. Or at least, not by using the same technology and the means of transport deployed by the original builders.

There is so much that cannot be explained by the current narrative, however desperate folk may be to cling on to it.

For when one questions the anomalies and contradictions in the official record, and looks through a fresh pair of eyes, there is far too much evidence (circumstantial or otherwise) to dismiss the distinct possibility that something world changing happened in the not too distant past.

Prior to the 19th and early 20th century, architecture displays much the same principles all over the world, that we now call classical Greco-Roman architecture. Why did this style of building stop?

Why are there so many colossal stone buildings located in all major cities around the world, of such intricate architectural design, which seem oddly out of place in their immediate surroundings?

City tour guides have been trained to parrot the mainstream

historical narrative, blissfully unaware that much has been falsified.

Whilst we take their presence for granted, every year, millions of tourists and visitors will often travel hundreds, or even thousands of miles just to see them with their own eyes and take photographs of these grand structures. Then turn and say;

"They just don't build them like this any more, do they?".

But someone did build them of course, however they managed it, and satisfied with this brief flash of inspiration, the tourists return home with their collection of snapshots.

Why do we see so many late nineteenth century photos of cities like Moscow, New York, London and Paris, their infrastructure glorious, and let's be honest, the people and their means of transport primitive, unsophisticated, and without the means to build a city like this?

Yet at the same time, we also see simpler, far less refined buildings which align with the people. Charming in their own way, but coarse with their use of wood, simple brick and plaster. Exactly the type of architecture one would expect to find with a generation living in the horse and cart era. Effectively, we see architectural evidence for the old world and the modern world, in the same photograph, but think little or nothing of it.

Early photographs of Moscow and St Petersburg, show the cities were enormous, and could likely hold a population well into the millions. Why then, in the 1800's, were these cities so vast if the population was only 300,000 to 500,000 in each at the time? In fact, we see pretty much deserted cities grow to bustling cities within 20 years or so. It makes for little sense.

Unless of course, an event had taken place which reduced the population numbers. Could this be the reason why there is in these photographs, such a stark contrast between a lack of population, and the sheer size of the city buildings?

I recently watched an old black and white movie (with some added colour) filmed from the front of a moving tram, probably in the late nineteenth or early twentieth century. It is by far the most surreal, city sight-seeing trip I've ever taken.

Filmed in Brussels, virtually everybody out and about is wearing dark clothing. Although a few of the ladies are wearing a white blouse, all have long black skirts which are sweeping the ground. Like a scene from an old Charlie Chaplin movie, all the gentlemen, many with walking canes tucked under their arm, are dressed in dark suits with matching black hats.

When comparing the size of the people in the film footage with the grand and colossal buildings around them, it becomes glaringly noticeable that many have 15-20 feet tall entrance doorways, and the height of the stories measure 12 feet or more. Something is not right here, for at times it almost appears that these people were picking up, from where a previous people of a much larger stature, left off.

Some refer to these people as the Reset Generation, those who seem to have appeared on the scene, as if out of nowhere. This sudden appearance however, is more likely due to the advent of the movie camera. Either way, the people in these early photographs certainly seem out of sync with the architectural grandeur and the sheer size of the imposing buildings which surround them.

Wanton Destruction

Over the last few centuries, the true purpose of these architectural wonders has been systematically concealed, and the physical evidence of a former, advanced technology has gradually been removed. At the same time, hundreds of thousands of the old world structures, have been deliberately destroyed.

Many of the old buildings which couldn't be removed are now churches, post offices, government buildings, cinemas and theatres.

It's reckoned that Tokyo had well in excess of 2,500 of these old world buildings till around the mid nineteenth century. The massive 7.9 magnitude Kanto earthquake of September 1, 1923, fires and the Japanese government have since destroyed the majority of these old world constructions.

The two World Wars, especially WWII, played a major role in erasing much of the old world infrastructure from our cities in an act of wanton destruction. Dresden in Germany, which was originally designed as a Star City, was by all accounts, filled with amazing architecture.

To this day, war historians remain uncertain of Winston Churchill's true motive for the strategic fire bombing of Dresden on February 13, 1945. Historians maintain Churchill's motives were political rather than military, and unanimously agree that Dresden had no military value. Not one military unit, not one anti-aircraft battery was deployed in the city.

Yet 722 heavy bombers of the British Royal Air Force, and 527 of the United States Army Air Forces dropped more than 3,900 tons of high-explosive bombs and incendiary devices on the city. An estimated 700,000 phosphorus bombs (one bomb for every 2 living souls) were dropped on 1.2 million people.

By the following day, more than 75% of the city, along with its inhabitants, was reduced to ashes and rubble, having been razed to the ground. The strategic fire bombing of Dresden, was the worst single massacre of all time, killing more people than Hiroshima and Nagasaki combined.

The most honourable Winston Churchill, was duly rewarded for playing his part in the mass murder of human life, and the wanton destruction of so much of the old world infrastructure. He was given a Knighthood and named 'Time' Magazine's Man of the Year in 1940 and 1949.

Allied bombers also killed tens of thousands, and destroyed large areas of city buildings with the attacks on Cologne, Hamburg and Berlin, each formerly a star city. And of course, the Japanese cities of Tokyo, Hiroshima and Nagasaki.

Likewise, the German Luftwaffe dropped thousands of bombs on London during the Blitz, from 1939 to 1945, killing almost 30,000 people. More than 70,000 buildings were completely demolished, and another 1.7 million were damaged. *(Credit Wikipedia.)*

Some of the surviving old world structures were repurposed as Post Offices, theatres, opera houses, town halls or government buildings.

Who knows what else has been done to accomplish all of this destruction. There is so much more to be accounted for, due to the amount of fabrication and whitewash.

Could it be possible that the controllers of the narrative had a dual agenda? What if two world wars were deemed necessary in order to introduce Zionism, and to create the modern-day state of Israel? For the sole purpose of falsifying Biblical end-times prophesy, by following the blueprint of Scripture?

Yet on the other hand, what if two world wars were deemed necessary in order to destroy any physical evidence for the past fulfilment of Biblical prophecy?

Although highly speculative, I'm now beginning to think this is most likely to be the case.

Much of the old world infrastructure in Iraq, was destroyed during the Gulf Wars. Under the Blair-Bush duo's false pretext of Saddam Hussein's non-existent stockpile of weapons of mass destruction.

Some researchers maintain there is even tantalizing evidence that the American Civil War was at least partially a cover up for the destruction of thousands of old world structures, and even a possible mudflood clean up.

So what may have happened in the past that has been covered up? A record of an unknown civilization who once ruled the Earth?

A Mud flood? A Great Reset of sorts? Or just one strange coincidence after another? An interesting rabbit hole indeed.

To quote the words of gifted researcher and documentary producer Jon Levi;

"To be lied to once is disturbing enough, but when we accept one lie, we inadvertently give permission for another followed by another until it reaches a point when our reality begins to look more like a science fiction show."

Mud-flood

Probably set in the 1830s, Charles Dickens writes in the opening chapter of his 1852 novel 'Bleak House'. *(Italics, mine)*.

> LONDON. Michaelmas Term lately over, and the Lord Chancellor sitting in Lincoln's Inn Hall. Implacable November weather. *As much mud in the streets* as if the waters had but newly retired from the face of the earth, and it would not be wonderful to meet a Megalosaurus, forty feet long or so, waddling like an elephantine lizard up Holborn Hill.
>
> Dogs, undistinguishable *in mire*. Horses, scarcely better; splashed to their very blinkers. Foot passengers, jostling one another's umbrellas in a general infection of ill-temper, and losing their foot-hold at street-corners, where tens of thousands of other foot passengers *have been slipping and sliding* since the day broke (if the day ever broke), adding new deposits *to the crust upon crust of mud,* sticking at those points tenaciously to the pavement, and *accumulating at compound interest.*

This is a fictitious story, and doesn't prove anything of course. But it certainly suggests that excessive amounts of mud in the streets of London at the time, was not an unusual sight.

The UK is renowned for its thousands of sites where ancient Roman architecture has been discovered over the centuries. The latest being the partial remains of a 1,700 year old Roman villa, found buried beneath eight feet of soil on family owned farmland in the summer of 2020, in Rutland County in the East Midlands of England.

When you start looking at some of the explanations for why all these architectural ruins are buried beneath several feet of dirt in a land not prone to volcanic eruption, earthquakes etc. it can get quite interesting. Whilst severe flooding due to a nearby river bursting its banks would be quite plausible, one English history site tells us;

> When the Romans left Britain, it appears that some villas were covered with dirt to 'trap' into them the spirits of the Romans – thus, they could not 'escape'.

The truth is, old buildings, which in many cases are buried beneath up to 20 feet of soil, have been discovered on every continent on Earth. Parts of Rome itself were buried in 20 to 40 feet of sediment which we're told was due to the aqueduct system being in disrepair, hence the entire area got flooded.

As mentioned, some explanations (if given) are actually quite plausible, whereas others are based on guesswork. But could there be a common factor for all of this?

Liquefaction

The phenomenon known as soil liquefaction commonly referred to as mud-flood, occurs when a cohesion-less, saturated or partially saturated soil, substantially loses strength and stiffness in response to an applied stress such as shaking during an earthquake or other sudden change in stress condition. (*Credit:Wikipedia.*)

Under these circumstances, material that is ordinarily a solid behaves like a liquid; much like an area of treacherous quicksand. Once the stress has subsided the soil begins to return to a solid state and in the aftermath we see fully, or part buried structures, buildings tilted at an angle, and uneven muddy streets where there was once tarmac or paving.

Mud can rise rapidly and dramatically with a destructive force which is unstoppable, causing massive landslides, affecting dams and bridges, and devastating entire areas of land, and in the worst case scenario entire cities may be destroyed.

The New Madrid Earthquakes of 1811-1812, are often brushed over or barely gain a mention in textbooks. After the February 7, 1812 earthquake, "boatmen reported that the Mississippi actually ran backwards for several hours". (*Credit:Wikipedia.*)

Although the 3 main earthquakes occurred in the central Mississippi Valley, they were felt as far away as New York City, Boston, Montreal, and Washington D.C. The thousands of after shocks which followed, even caused soil liquefaction in parts of the Central United States. (*credit:Wikipedia.*)

The June,16, 1964 Niigata earthquake in central Japan caused widespread liquefaction as too did the Alaska earthquake which occurred the same year. Most of the city's 5-storey apartment blocks became quite steeply inclined and one of them was completely overturned.

Soil liquefaction was a major factor in the destruction of San Francisco's Marina District during the 1989 Loma Prieta earthquake, and in the Japanese Port of Kobe during the 1995 Great Hanshin earthquake. (*credit:Wikipedia.*)

Liquefaction was largely responsible for the extensive damage to residential properties and the infrastructure of the eastern suburbs in the vicinity of Christchurch, New Zealand, during the 2010 Canterbury earthquake, and more extensively again following the earthquakes in early to mid-2011. Some of the photographs show entire streets all partially buried in volumes of thick, gooey mud. Most vehicles are completely submerged, whilst others have only a small portion of the roof showing.

The Great East Japan Earthquake of 2011 caused unprecedented damage. Even areas 300 kilometres away from the epicentre suffered damages beyond what was predicted. Soil liquefaction occurred over a large area. Some 27,000 structures sank or tilted, causing massive damage.

On 28 September, 2018, an earthquake of 7.5 magnitude hit the Central Sulawesi province of Indonesia. Resulting soil liquefaction buried the suburb of Balaroa and Petobo village under almost 10 feet of mud. The Indonesian Government is considering designating the two neighbourhoods of Balaroa and Petobo, that have been totally buried under mud, as a mass grave site.

So yes, soil liquefaction, which can result in an unstoppable, fast flowing river of mud burying everything in its path is a well documented phenomena.

A similar phenomena known as Mud Boils, which are volcano-like cones of fine sand and silt that range from several inches to several feet high and from several inches to more than 30 feet in diameter. Active mud boils are dynamic ebb-and-flow features that can erupt and form a large cone in several days, then cease flowing, or they may discharge continuously for several years. They have been observed in the Tully Valley in Onondaga County, in central New York State, since the late 1890s. *(Credit: Wikipedia.)*

Mud or sand boils that emerge from asphalt roads, cause cars and buildings to start sinking, topple over or collapse.

Localized mud-floods are not that uncommon, but mud-floods occurring simultaneously in multiple nations within the same time period should be considered extremely rare.

Yet could it be possible that an earth-shaking event causing soil liquefaction which resulted in a devastating mud-flood occurred in the not too distant past? One which drastically affected numerous locations across the earth simultaneously?

One positive aspect of soil liquefaction is the tendency for the effects of earthquake shaking to be significantly reduced, thus shock-waves are less likely to be transferred to buildings at the ground surface. This could explain why the buildings in many towns and villages which appear to have been affected by mud-flood in the past, were partially buried but not actually destroyed in the process.

Easter Island in the southeastern Pacific Ocean, is famed for the overly large stone heads, which stand like sentinels around its perimeter. It wasn't until 2012 when it was discovered that the 834 visible heads only made up for about three-eighths of the statues size.

With soil liquefaction as a possible cause, the 834 stone torsos and bodies which make up the bulk of the statues, were found buried upright beneath the ground.

There are at least thirteen leaning towers around the world, for which soil liquefaction is a possible cause. The very fact the leaning tower of Pizza is still standing, albeit at an angle, after surviving soil liquefaction, is proof of how advanced the structural engineering and construction methods of the time were.

Why can so many old photographs from the late 19th century be found on the Internet of pretty much deserted towns and cities, with streets littered with debris, dirt and mud? Some show huge mounds of soil and deep, gaping trenches being excavated in residential areas, which are maybe 75 or more yards in length, and 12-15 feet deep.

Many such images show teams of workmen clearing large mounds of soil, levelling the ground, and in some cases, seem to be excavating the lower two or three lower levels of existing structures. The perspective some of these photos provide, clearly show the surrounding streets are at least 15-20 feet higher than they were originally.

Yet we are often given no official explanation to justify such excavations, nor the huge amounts of dirt and mud we see. These photos also suggest that whatever the cause, something had happened in the fairly recent past.

The complete absence of a reasonable mainstream justification for the buried architecture and vast amounts of mud and dirt that we see, suggests that the controllers are deliberately trying to hide whatever happened in the past.

Photographs from Crimea around the end of the nineteenth century show streets buried by 9 to 12 feet of mud and clay, and the lower floors of buildings and pavements12 feet or more below ground level. The image below is a screenshot from the documentary, "Lost History of the Flat Earth."

As can be seen by the mud-line running along the entire length of the building, the surrounding streets were recently buried beneath 12 feet of mud.

Where did all this excess mud come from?

I recently viewed a similar photograph, taken in Russia I believe, of the front of a 2-storey house, including the front door. The street out front had been excavated to reveal the previously buried front door and a couple of windows of the original ground floor level. It is evident from the photograph, that rather than clear all the excess mud, an extra 2 storeys were added to the original ground floor.

In fact there are numerous examples of old buildings that have been excavated showing previously hidden lower levels.

Where did all this extra mud/dirt come from?

Many late 19th century images can be found of cities in eastern Europe and Russia, which show deserted streets that appear to have been levelled and with much of the mud removed.

It is estimated that in many cases, prior to removal the layer of excess mud in the streets was on average around 3 feet deep.

Often these photographs of unrefined and muddy streets are set against a backdrop of refined, sophisticated and magnificent architecture. Could these cities have suffered a similar fate of soil liquefaction that we have seen in more recent times?

Perhaps, but realistically, muddy roads is not enough to base any conclusions on.

It could also be argued of course, that seemingly deserted towns and cities, was likely the result of the long delayed exposure time of the earliest cameras. For unless people remained stationary for the duration of the exposure, they probably wouldn't appear in the photo. At the same time however, there is also a noticeable absence of hand-carts and wagons parked up, of the type used by street vendors and delivery men etc. that one might expect to see in the cities. And it wouldn't explain why many of the streets look filthy and littered with debris, almost as though they had recently been awash with mud.

Some claim such photos of empty cities, were taken in the early morning hours, before local residents were up and about. The problem here is, the angle and length of the shadows in some of the images, which indicate the photos were taken closer to, or around midday.

One thing is certain, whoever took these photographs of deserted cities, especially those which show a panoramic view of the entire area, done so with intent. The viewer is meant to see it.

Whatever the case, to see images of these empty towns, is actually quite disturbing. In some ways they remind me of my home town during the first Lockdown, only far worse. At least I saw a handful of people in the streets, albeit most looking rather bewildered as they peered at me from over the top of their mask.

And why are there so many old residential buildings that have lower floor windows situated below, or mostly below ground level with only the top section of glass visible from outside? I'm sure we've all seen them at some point in our lives.

There are even a number of old churches and other buildings, with the sunken windows, and in some cases doorways, entirely below ground level. Were they built with an entrance or window partially, or even below ground?

Or were they originally constructed prior to a localized mud-flood, the aftermath of which, raised the ground level of the area surrounding them? Making the original ground floor now appear to be the basement?

One is hard pushed to find any photos which show the construction of these possible mud-flood buildings.

I've been told by a Ukrainian, now living in England, that many of the buildings in his former home town, have the first floor underground. At first glance, he says, it's not always easy to tell, because they have been remodelled. But if you look at some of the old abandoned buildings, you can clearly see the doors and windows of the first floor are beneath the level of the roads.

Evidently, much of Russia is the same.

Investigative researchers have even discovered many old buildings in American cities with 2 or more floors below street level. One researcher describes them as being;

"quite elaborate, with decorative brick arches in what are supposed to be sewers and cellars—and seemingly intentionally ruined".

More often than not, the buried masonry etc. is consistent with the architecture seen in the buildings above ground.

Some photos show Russia's Winter Palace, the US Capitol Building, and New York's St Mary Magdalene church, having been completely dug out around the base, to reveal lower levels than were previously known about.

A simple Google search will let you see at least a dozen of these buildings. But once you see this sunken infrastructure which is so prevalent across the earth, you can never un-see it. One has to question why there are so many photographs of entire lower levels of buildings being dug out, with no explanation as why they were submerged in the earth in the first place?

To help put things into perspective, numerous black and white photographs from the nineteenth century can be found of various cities across the world, with primitive dirt streets, and pedestrians, or workmen standing alongside horse and carts, with impossible buildings towering in the background.

Why spend what must have amounted to a small fortune, to erect such elaborate and costly structures, when the roads surrounding them are so basic by comparison, and the local residents appear to be so relatively poor?

Time and again we see old photographs of unrefined and dirty streets, simple, terraced dwellings and poverty, with magnificent regal buildings standing in the background. In fact, complete with Gothic spires, and huge columns adorning their marble-stepped entrances, they tend to stick out like a sore thumb, compared with the majority of buildings around them. Once again, there appears to be two conflicting stories in the same narrative.

Rarely, if ever, can photographs be found, of these buildings under construction. To be fair, the occasional old photograph of workmen wielding a shovel, or accompanied by a horse and cart, are not evidence of anything.

Could these elaborate grand structures, which seem so out of place in their local surroundings, have been erected prior to a massive mud-flood, and have since been reclaimed and renovated? I don't know the answer either, but have my suspicions and feel it's worth thinking about.

There's an official explanation for nearly everything of course, but time and again, anomalies can be seen in many old photographs that seem bizarrely out of character, especially for the time period they were supposedly built in. In the main, an official explanation is merely a cover story. A cover story being a story that conceals some other atrocity or catastrophe by hiding the real cause of the atrocity.

As it stands, the argument for a worldwide Mud-Flood is relatively weak, yet it is probably unwise to dismiss the possibility of soil liquefaction occurring at multiple locations across the realm simultaneously.

For although the Scriptures doesn't actually mention a mud-flood, they describe earth-shaking events, which we are told are the main contributing factor for Soil Liquefaction.

On three occasions the Bible records how God will shake the heavens and earth, and a time is foretold when the foundations of the earth will shake, be moved exceedingly, and reel to and fro like a drunkard. *(Reference;Isaiah 24:18-20.)*

Haggai 2:6. For thus saith the LORD of hosts; Yet once, it is a little while, and I will shake the heavens, and the earth, and the sea, and the dry land;

So yes, in light of Bible prophecy, catastrophic mud-floods affecting multiple nations simultaneously, certainly cannot be ruled out.

Loess

Wikipedia describe the natural phenomena known as loess, as being a wind-borne sediment consisting of grain-sized particles of rock, clay, sand and silt that covers around ten percent of Earth's entire land surface area. Loess deposits, which can range in depth or thickness, from a single decimetre to several tens of metres, are widely distributed across many provinces in China, and are found across the entire European continent.

Evidently loess can easily be removed with a shovel, yet at the same time is firm enough to be carved out to form a simple cave dwelling, known in China as a yaodong or "house cave". In 2006, an estimated 40 million people in northern China lived in yaodongs.

Beneath the old German town of Oppenheim, famous for its wine production, there exists approximately two hundred kilometres of connected tunnels and wine cellars, dug laterally through the thick bed of loess.

In North America loess covers the plains of the Platte, Missouri, Mississippi, and Ohio rivers and the Columbia Plateau. In fact, loess deposits of varying thickness can be found in most all nations on Earth.

We are told that dependent upon the force of wind energy, these deeper or thicker layers of loess, have gradually accumulated *"over a sufficient amount of time,"* although according to Wikipedia, it's reckoned the loess deposits in North America, are less than 30,000 years old.

I'm not a geologist, but is it possible that in some areas of the U.S. much of the loess has been deposited very rapidly in far more recent times?

For why are there photos of a number of buildings constructed 150 or so years ago in Kansas, that are surrounded by huge mounds of loess deposits known as bluffs, which stand up to 50 feet tall or more?

The obvious answer would be that the buildings were erected in the vicinity of these vertical mounds of soil. Yet whilst numerous old photographs from the 1860's can be found of roads being dug out and levelled in the proximity of buildings, to find a photograph of an actual building under construction is extremely rare.

Thus far in fact, I've not been able to find a single one.

Birth of a City

According to Wikipedia; "the Great Flood of 1844 is the biggest flood ever recorded on the Missouri River and Upper Mississippi River, in North America, in terms of discharge."

Among the hardest hit in terms of mortality were the Wyandot Indians, who lost 100 people in a cholera epidemic that occurred after the flood in the vicinity of today's Kansas City, Kansas.

The flood also caused settlers to go further west to Westport Landing in Kansas City, *"which resulted in significant local economic and cultural impact."*

According to Dr. Richard Gentile, Professor Emeritus of Geology at the University of Missouri-Kansas City, the old settlement town of Kansas at the time, was virtually washed away by the flood, and had to be completely rebuilt.

According to Wikipedia, Kansas was incorporated as a town on June 1, 1850, and as a city on March 28, 1853.

By 1857, and having started from scratch in 1844, Dr. Gentile records that the town of Kansas had;

> 40 manufacturers, including 5 saw mills, 3 brick yards, 2 grain mills, blacksmith and wagon makers, 16 hotels, 26 salons and a large number of gambling houses. The population was estimated to be 4,000.

Far be it from me to question the expertise of a fully qualified geologist, and a Professor Emeritus to boot, but that many premises, including 40 manufacturers and 16 hotels, seems an incredible achievement over a period of 13 years.

Especially when his own personal collection of photographs taken in the late 1860's, appear to tell a completely different story. Rather than being a thriving town, it is virtually empty, with just a handful of pedestrians and the occasional mule or two wandering the streets.

From all accounts, the terrain the city was built on was a hostile and barren environment, consisting of steep hills, gorges and ravines. Furthermore, much of the limestone bedrock was buried beneath a thick blanket of loess.

By the 1860's, developers had cut through the big limestone bluffs that had been deterrents to southern expansion of the city from the river area.

A collection of astounding photographs taken in Kansas City, Missouri, back in the Spring of 1867, show 3-storey buildings erected on limestone bedrock, whilst the huge mounds of loess around them, are in the process of being dug out.

I do find it strange however, that of all the available photographs of streets being levelled, and completed buildings, there is a noticeable absence of buildings under construction.

For the closest to a building actually in the process of being constructed, that I've been able to find, is an old black and white photograph taken in 1869, and bearing the caption;

> Removing the blanket of loess. The site is being graded for construction of the Nelson Hotel, Northeastern corner of 2nd and Main streets June 1869.

One photograph shows the magnificent 4-storey Gilliss House Hotel, which was designed with two 4-storey wings separated by a 5-storey central tower, which is topped with an octagonal cupola. In fact it looks remarkably like an old world structure, hence more likely to have been an inherited building.

Built in the 1850's or so we are told, the Gilliss House stands on a thick layer of limestone bedrock, whilst the huge mounds of soil in the foreground have been dug out to street level.

The official story maintains that the streets were being graded, or lowered at the time. Yet although one cannot be certain, it appears from the photo that the street already existed, and was actually in the process of being excavated.

The depth of the trench is around 20 feet, which can be reasonably estimated due to the men with their horses and covered wagons, busy with shovels at the base of the excavation site. Meaning, if indeed the streets were already present at that time, they had previously been buried beneath 20 or more feet of soil.

One of Dr. Richard Gentile's extraordinary photographs (number 25) shows a small section of the left hand wall and the entire frontage, along with part of the apex roof of the large 2-storey Mechanics Bank Building.

It appears that the main street out front, and the entire right hand side of the building has already been cleared or excavated. For the summit of the huge stack of soil piled high against both the left hand side and the rear of the building, far exceeds the height of both storeys plus the capped ridge running along the top of the sloping roof.

There are no photographs, or none that I've been able to find anyway, of the Mechanics Bank under construction. So the question is, was this large 2-storey building deliberately erected flush against the huge vertical bluff, standing both alongside and behind it?

Or does the photograph reveal an entire building being exhumed from the grave, so to speak? A building found buried beneath hundreds of tons of loess and in the process of being excavated? If so this is hidden history at its finest, and revealed in an early photograph.

As far as I can figure there could only be two possible reasons for this. *1)*. The construction of the Mechanics Bank was completed by the early settlers, who in their haste, had not bothered to excavate at least half of the loess surrounding it.

2). The early settlers had discovered buildings that should not have been there. Old world structures found buried beneath hundreds of tons of loess. The photograph was taken in 1867 as the excavation work was underway, but still only half completed.

Either way, logic dictates that buildings cannot possibly be buried in soil without having been constructed beforehand.

In an article titled *"The rock ledge along the Missouri River that gave birth to Kansas City"*, Dr. Richard Gentile offers the following strange information;

> Dr. Lester, a physician, had an office on Main Street between 2nd and 3rd street. He left for a week, and during his absence, the street was graded and lowered 10 feet. He just added another floor. One year later the street was lowered another 12 feet. He just added another floor. Thus, he built a 3-story office building from the top down.

What does " building from the top down" even mean? The more I read it, the less sense it makes. For if the street out front of any building is lowered by 10 feet, it will make no difference whatsoever to the height of that building.

A 3-storey building will remain a 3-storey building regardless of workmen digging holes in the street.

Overall, the article itself is highly informative concerning the early history of Kansas city, and the author has quite a remarkable collection photographs from the mid to late 1800's.

Then we are introduced to Dr. Lester, who in 1867, somehow managed to "build a 3-story office building from the top down".

 Maybe it was said "tongue in cheek", so to speak. Who knows? But I certainly find statements of such nature intriguing.

Could this be an attempt to explain why the third level of the building was the first to fully appear from the soil during the excavation work? That rather than building from the top down, the workmen excavated the building from the top down?

But somehow, these early settlers without the funding, resources, or skills, erected buildings that rivalled old world architecture in practically no time at all.

For suddenly, and as if out of nowhere, we're told that the iconic 4-storey Diamond Building was completed in Kansas City in 1870. Photographs of the building show a highly sophisticated structure, with a French-style Mansard Roof, that being a roof with two slopes on all four sides.

This magnificent building, which is totally alien to the timeline presented by the official narrative, was demolished in 1915. By "totally alien", I mean the grand architectural style of the building looks completely out of character within its surroundings.

It was even referred to by the Kansas City Times (Feb.9/2020) as being a 'Diamond in the Rough.'

As mentioned earlier, there were many strange things going on in the nineteenth century, that we have not been informed of. Instead, we have been presented with a fabricated, or at best, sanitised narrative. The controllers do not want folk to question the narrative and think for themselves. At the same time they become complacent, knowing full well that few will believe the folk who do take the time to question the narrative.

To quote the Greek philosopher, Plato;

"Those who are able to see beyond the shadows and lies of their culture will never be understood, let alone believed, by the masses".

The Insane and the Orphan

Officially, the time of the Industrial Revolution was the transition to new manufacturing processes in Great Britain, continental Europe, and the United States, in the period from about 1760 to sometime between 1820 and 1840.

On their website, 'Stolen History' notes that;

> During the course of industrialization during the 19th century, far-reaching social changes occurred in the Western world. The extent of these changes has not yet been adequately understood. Aspects such as rural flight, mass impoverishment, orphanages, lack of hygiene in the cities and related epidemics are known in historical research, but these are only the effects of the Industrial Revolution. A more elusive topic has been the question what caused the massive technological upheavals of the 19th century. So far, the two most important questions have not been answered sufficiently: Why did the Industrial Revolution begin in England, and why precisely around 1800?

> If you break it down to its essence, the Industrial Revolution consisted of ground-breaking technological inventions that permanently changed social life, and enabled increasing automation of production. In particular, the development of the steam engine supposedly laid the foundation for the further development of electric and internal combustion engines, which form the foundation of today's society.

> The Industrial Revolution presents us with a conundrum. In terms of the official narrative, humanity bumbled along at a low state of development for thousands of years, only to suddenly undergo a massive leap in development within a few decades without any apparent external cause.

> To make matters even more absurd, since the end of the industrial age, mankind has again found itself in a period of technological stagnation - the supposed inventive spirit of Central Europe and Germany in particular, which historians say made industrialization possible, seems to have vanished.

Unofficially, the 19th and early 20th century was a time of transition from the old world into the modern era. The old technology based on free energy was gradually being phased out, and replaced with the controlled release of technologies which rely on scarce and hard-to-get resources, allowing the ruling powers to gain a monopoly on the energy supply and the production of goods.

At the same time, thousands of old world buildings were being repurposed or demolished. This time period roughly corresponds with what is termed the "Age of Enlightenment", which officially ended in 1815.

The year 1816 was cold, wet, stormy and dark. It was the worst summer in living memory at that time, and not at all like typical summer weather. Consequently, 1816 became known in Europe and North America as 'The Year Without a Summer.'

Whether the year 1816 is relevant or not, I don't know, but it occurred just a few years before the Industrial Revolution began to reach a close.

We're told that the year without a summer was due to the massive volcanic eruption the previous year, of Mount Tambora in Indonesia. The sheer volume of volcanic ash particles ejected high into the stratosphere was so great, it caused average temperatures across the world to drop by three degrees Celsius.

This resulted in major crop failures due to frost and lack of sunshine, causing severe food shortages, especially across Europe, the United States and Canada. *(Adapted in part from UCAR;Center for Science Education.)*

1816 was the year Mary Shelley wrote *Frankenstein*, a horror novel set in an often cold, bleak and stormy environment. It was also the year Lord Byron wrote the poem *Darkness*, which begins with;

"I had a dream, which was not all a dream. The bright sun was extinguish'd." It would seem that Lord Byron's *dream, which was not all a dream,* was based upon his own personal experience.

Over roughly the same time period, there was a seemingly rapid and unexplained increase in the numbers of folk suffering from serious mental health issues, along with various other emotional or spiritual afflictions (including Epilepsy) across Great Britain, Continental Europe and the USA.

A 291 page report published in 1844 by The Lunacy Commission of England and Wales, records the seriousness of the problem, and labels the majority of those afflicted as being "Pauper lunatics."

Often referred to as "harmless idiots" many of these poor unfortunate souls were "farmed out", if not to a willing family member, then to

local peasants and small farmers, in exchange for a weekly allowance. This was the origin of the term, "to farm out".
According to the 1844 Welsh Report (p.11 /North Wales.)

> The condition of a considerable proportion of the pauper lunatics boarded or farmed out is bad, in many cases most miserable, and in nearly all such as to deprive them of the means or probability of cure by medical treatment.

For some afflicted with Epilepsy, or deemed to be harmful to others at times, a form of restraint was often required. The amount of restraint used was left to the discretion of the people the sufferer boarded with. This, and the lack of supervision, resulted in some atrocious cases. (*1844 Welsh Report, p.59.*)
Ann Abney of Buith near Bangor, for example:

> had been kept chained in the house of a married daughter, and, from having been long kept down in a crouching posture, her knees were forced up to her chin, and she sat wholly upon her hips and her heels, and much excoriation was caused upon her chest and stomach by her knees when she moved. She could move about with velocity, and was almost always maniacal. When she died [in Hereford Lunatic Asylum on 30.1.1844], it required very considerable dissection to get her pressed into a coffin.

The old census forms from 1851 in England have a section listing if anyone in the household is 1. Imbecile or idiot or 2. Lunatic, so they differentiated between them somehow.
Public mental asylums were established in Britain after the passing of the 1808 County Asylums Act. This empowered magistrates to build rate-supported asylums in every county to house the many 'pauper lunatics'. Nine counties first applied, and the first public asylum opened in 1812 in Nottinghamshire, known as the Nottingham General Lunatic Asylum.
The facility initially accommodated 80 patients, but as demand for places increased additional facilities were required, and it became necessary to augment capacity by establishing the Coppice Lunatic Hospital in 1859 and the Mapperley Asylum in 1880.
According to Wikipedia, the foundation stone of the Nottingham Lunatic Asylum was laid on 31 May 1810 and the first patients were admitted in February 1812.

I know Wikipedia is far from infallible and it may be a genuine mistake, but why claim the hospital was built in less than 2 years? Early engravings, sketches and paintings show it was a massive, well weathered and impressive 3 storey building with a row of eight individual chimney stacks, plus a basement level below ground.

Set in its own park-like surroundings with a fancy flight of steps leading up to the grand entrance, it appears far more like a stately residence than a hospital. Even today such a magnificent structure couldn't possibly be built in a couple of years, as was supposedly the case in 1810.

The same is true of Nottingham's Coppice and Mapperley Asylums, which complete with towers, cupolas and distinctive Renaissance characteristics, were built in the Italianate style.

In fact, the same is true of pretty much all of the 128 Lunatic Asylums that were established in the UK over the course of the nineteenth century. The majority of which have since been razed to the ground.

The Victorian era was a time of hardship and deprivation for the average family, and even young children were often expected to work. Yet we also see such over the top extravagance. Time and again, these two conflicting stories of poverty and exorbitance appear in the same narrative during the Victorian era.

Why were such a large number of huge, elaborate and no expense spared, mansions erected as Lunatic Asylums in the horse-drawn carriage, Victorian era? They weren't. Like the majority of the lunatic asylums in Britain, these grand buildings were more likely *inherited*, renovated and repurposed structures dating back to the previous era.

Between the passing of the Lunatic Asylums Act in 1845 and 1890, when the next act was passed, over sixty asylums were built and opened in London. A further forty were subsequently constructed.

Some people in prominent positions founded organizations with the aim of helping people find their way out of poverty and deplorable living conditions. At the same time providing the bare minimum of worthy or unworthy charitable aid.

This was also around the same time when the sale of alcoholic beverages became more widely available to the general public. Introduced primarily as a coping mechanism maybe?

Unfortunately, for many, lunatic asylums were regarded as prisons disguised as hospitals. It was a convenient way for the 'controllers' to remove the poor and incurable from society and for those with money, private madhouses were often convenient dumping grounds for unwanted wives. It was also a convenient way for governments to rid society of those they considered trouble makers and dissidents. Although many patients were admitted for short periods of time, there are plenty of horror stories of patients who were admitted to asylums, often for very unsatisfactory reasons, and basically locked up and forgotten about. Some could spend twenty or more years locked away, and sadly an unnecessary high number of patients died without ever being released.

No doubt many are familiar with the abundance of horror stories concerning the deplorable conditions and the horrific treatment of patients in mental asylums. Reports of patients being abused, poorly fed and beaten, left chained in outhouses without heating, and wallowing in filth for years, are sadly not uncommon.

America

A similar pattern was unfolding in America. According to Dr. Benjamin Rush, the "father of American Psychiatry," asylums in the US went from having a couple of hundred patients to thousands. In the 1820's, on average, 57 patients were admitted to each asylum. In the 1870's, that number rose to 473. *(Credit:Wikipedia.)*

Again, these massive institutional buildings were seemingly erected in a relatively short space of time and apparently with no expense spared. The New York State Lunatic Asylum at Utica for example, which opened on January 16, 1843.

With its grand entrance supported by six 48 feet tall columns each 8 feet in diameter, the structure itself stands over 50 feet (15m) high, 550 feet (170m) long, and nearly 50 feet (15m) in depth.

This architectural marvel which resembled the Brandenburg Gate in Berlin, and was constructed in the Greek Revival style, was known as the 'The Old Main'.

Yet again, we are left to ponder on the deliberate but unnecessary extravagance? Not in the least because much of the Old Main was destroyed by fire in 1852 through an act of arson, just nine years after construction. Needless to say, demolition of the grand entrance building soon followed.

Founded, so we're told in 1838, the Columbus State Hospital, also known as the Lunatic Asylum of Ohio, was said to have been the largest building in the U.S. or the world, until the Pentagon was completed in 1943. (Credit:Wikipedia.)

This massive, remodelled old world structure, complete with domes, towers and antennae, was destroyed by fire in 1868.

Much like stories that emerged in Britain, the Utica asylum, among others, was said to have staff members that performed lobotomies and electroshock therapy quite regularly on patients. Over the years, stories of deplorable living conditions were told, with many claiming that the patients who resided here received hardly any care and were left confined in small quarters.

It wasn't until the horrific conditions at these mental health facilities were exposed through undercover investigations and a number of patient witnesses, that they were finally brought to light.

Foundlings

Oddly enough, this rapid and in the main unexplained explosion of severe mental health, emotional and spiritual issues afflicting so many folk in Britain and America in the mid 19th-century, roughly corresponds with the time period when millions of orphans seem to have mysteriously appeared worldwide, almost as if out of thin air.

There are a number of given reasons for this, such as poverty, disease, overcrowding in the home, babes born out of wedlock, the death of a parent etc.

Although each of these reasons are certainly valid, even collectively, they really don't seem to justify the massive and almost overnight increase in the number of orphans.

In 1834, the British Government introduced 'The New Poor Act' which ended parish relief for unmarried mothers and allowed fathers of illegitimate children to avoid paying for child support. Unmarried mothers then received little assistance and the poor were left with no other option, than to enter the workhouse, or prostitution.

This harsh treatment inflicted on single mothers, coupled with the social stigma attached, forced many to give up their child to the local authorities.

Maternal instinct apart, there was certainly no incentive for women to become pregnant at the time.

According to 'Statista', the child mortality rate in Britain at the time for children under the age of five, was 329 deaths per thousand births. This means that approximately one in every three children born in the mid 1800's did not make it to their fifth birthday.

I've no wish to appear heartless, but in the cold light of day, without this high 33% mortality rate, the overall number of orphans would likely have been exceedingly higher.

Thus, it should come as no particular surprise that many of the most memorable characters in 19th century literature, turn out to be orphans. Oliver Twist, David Copperfield, Pip Pirrip, Jane Eyre, Heathcliff, Catherine Earnshaw, Jude Fawley and Tom Sawyer are just some of the many well-known literary characters in the Victorian era.

Wrote Charles Dickens in an extract from his nineteenth century novel, 'Little Dorrit';

> ...the originator of the Institution for these poor foundlings
> having been a blessed creature of the name of Coram, we gave
> that name to Pet's little maid. At one time she was Tatty, and at
> one time she was Coram and now she is always Tattycoram.

It's historically recognized that the former sea farer, Thomas Coram (c.1668-March 29, 1751), having frequently been shocked by the sight of infants exposed in the streets of London, often in a dying state, was responsible for the original foundling hospitals.

After 17 years of tireless campaigning, Thomas Coram finally received a Royal Charter from King George II in 1739, enabling him to establish the Bloomsbury Foundling Hospital in 1741, to care for and educate some of London's most vulnerable children.

Coram first obtained a lease on a property in Hatton Garden that could take 30 vulnerable infants. On 25 March 1741, the first babies at risk of abandonment were admitted to the institution's temporary home. Illegitimate infants had to be under 12 months of age, and were admitted after the mother had been interviewed and deemed to meet the criteria set out by the hospital.

Once they had been accepted, children were registered, often under a new identity, and were sent to live with a 'nurse' or foster family in the country. When they reached four or five years of age, children were sent to live at the Foundling Hospital in London where they received schooling until they were 15 years old, and then were apprenticed, usually to work in domestic or military service.

For in the meanwhile, Thomas Coram had purchased a 56 acre site in Bloomsbury, London, from the Earl of Salisbury. The building we're told was designed by architect Theodore Jacobsen, and we're told the founding stone of the new purpose-built Bloomsbury Foundling Hospital, which was surrounded by fields, was laid in September 1742.

Thus far I've been unable to find any information regarding the construction of the Foundling Hospital, not even from the UK Government National Archives. There are numerous engravings, sketches and paintings of the original building available, however.

Like many other orphanages at the time, this palatial building with its elaborate architecture, and set in its own sumptuous, park-like surroundings, was visually stunning. Again, why such over the top extravagance?

Quite frankly, there is no way this massive building was constructed over a couple of years as the narrative suggests. Such extraordinary buildings constructed in the alleged given time period, only make some sort of sense if they already existed. Yet another example of old world structures being *inherited*, restored and redefined maybe, this time to meet the growing orphan crisis?

From 1741 when the first babies were admitted, to 1954 when the last pupil was placed in foster care, the Foundling Hospital cared for and educated around 25,000 children.

Why did well over 20,000 mothers hand over their children to this one foundling home alone? Was something else going on at the time? Did the government need vast numbers of young children for the purpose of relocating them to other countries? An international repopulation program? Is this why Europe sent millions of orphans and young children to other countries, primarily America?

And that's just the sanitized version, for stories of cruelty and abuse surrounding these orphanages are as abundant as those surrounding the mental health institutions.

John Lennon's 'Strawberry Fields Forever', where "nothing is real" and "living is easy with eyes closed" refers to the Salvation Army Orphanage, 'Strawberry Fields' in Liverpool, which closed down after seventy years of child abuse.

Wikipedia lists 143 orphanages founded in the UK during the 19th century, and the list is only partial. Like 'Strawberry Fields', virtually all have since closed down or been demolished. As too have the hundreds of lunatic asylums.

By comparison, Irish born philanthropist Thomas John Barnardo, founder and director of homes for poor and deprived children, took a more modest approach, by adopting the 'cottage homes' model. He believed that children could be best supported if they were living in small, family-style groups looked after by a house 'mother'.

By 1900, the Barkingside 'garden village' had 65 cottages, a school, a hospital and a church, which provided a home and training, to 1,500 girls.

From the foundation of the homes in 1867 to the date of Barnardo's death (19 September 1905) nearly 60,000 children had been taken in, most being trained and placed out in life. At the time of his death, his charity was caring for over 8,500 children in 96 homes. *(Credit:Wikipedia.)*

Orphan Trains

Meanwhile, across the Atlantic, America was experiencing a similar phenomena. New York city had 4 foundling hospitals that processed thousands of children annually. The American Civil War is said to have resulted in the need for even more orphanages with an estimated 400 thousand children needing placement.

The Orphan Asylum Society was established in New York City by philanthropists, Isabella Graham and Elizabeth Hamilton on March 15, 1806, and the cornerstone of their first orphanage in Greenwich Village was laid on July 7, 1807.

According to village preservation.org, in 1835 the Orphan Asylum Society purchased land in the Bloomingdale village, on Seventy-Fourth Street, where the construction of a new asylum began immediately, and was concluded in 1837.

Now, I realize an artist's impression cannot be taken as evidence, but nevertheless, an old, colourful wood carving of this orphanage, shows the impossibility of it being constructed within a couple of years.

A magnificent central structure with 3 huge arched windows set above the main entrance, and a 4 storey wing attached to either side, each having 12 front windows. Four towering stone columns, which neatly divide each section of the building, add the finishing touch.

Although not a builder myself, if this carving is true to detail, there's no way it could have been constructed in two years.

Even today with a mini JCB to excavate the footings and dig out the trenches, instal the drainage and plumbing, with ready mixed concrete delivered on site, a huge 4-towered, 4 storey building of such finery and splendour, could not be achieved in 2 years. Ask anyone in the construction industry; such a task completed within a couple of years would be impossible.

Old world structures on both sides of the Atlantic, were being repurposed as Lunatic Asylums and Orphanages; the same being true for Canada, Australia, and right across Europe.

In 1850, we're told there was an estimated number of up to 30,000 homeless, orphaned or abandoned children in New York City alone. At the time, New York City's population was only 500,000. *(Warren, Andrea. "The Orphan Train", Washington Post, 1998.)*

It's not easy to find a logical explanation as to why 6% of a city's entire population should be homeless or orphaned children. Or even why they were relocated in the first place.

The Orphan Train Movement was the brainchild of American philanthropist, Charles Loring Brace, who in 1853 founded the Children's Aid Society.

Largely funded by the Astor family, Brace's infamous Orphan Train Movement was a supervised welfare program that transported children from crowded Eastern cities of the United States to foster homes located largely in rural areas of the Midwest.

Not all were orphaned or abandoned however, some were the children of newly arrived immigrants, or the children of the poorest and most destitute families living in these cities.

Wrote one reporter in an article for the New York Daily Tribune, (*Wednesday, January 21, 1880);*

"No mother's tears were shed over the departing waifs, no father's counsel was given to the boys who were about to enter upon a new life."

That new life began for hundreds of thousands of children, many of them babies, when they were dressed in new clothes, given a Bible, and placed in the care of Children's Aid Society agents, who then accompanied them west on trains called 'orphan trains' or 'mercy trains.'

Safeguards were put in place for lip service, but the reality was there were only a small handful of agents to monitor thousands of placements. Accompanied by CAS agent, E. P. Smith, the first group of 45 children arrived in Dowagiac, in the state of Michigan, on October 1, 1854. Stopping at various cities along the way, the children had travelled for days in uncomfortable conditions. *(Credit:Wikipedia.)*

Officially there were 97 institutions involved with orphans and the orphan trains. The Children's Aid Society sent an average of 3,000 children via train each year from 1855 to 1875. Orphan trains were sent to 45 states, as well as Canada and Mexico.

Whether true or not I wouldn't know, but there are even stories of babies and young children being shipped from state to state via the Postal Service.

With some journeys lasting several days, young children were transported right across the country, where they stopped at various cities, each having posters on display, announcing the arrival of the orphan train. When the train stopped, many children went to live with families that had placed orders beforehand, specifying age, gender, and hair and eye colour.

Writes Andrea Warren in an article for the *Washington Post, (1998.)*

> Few children understood what was happening at the time, but once they did, their reactions ranged from delight at finding a new family, to anger and resentment at being "placed out" when they had relatives back home.

The rest of the children were effectively paraded into the local hall or other venue designated as the "place of distribution." A polite way of saying a cattle market perhaps? For according to Sara Jane Richter, professor of history at Oklahoma Panhandle State University, the children often had unpleasant experiences. "People came along and prodded them, and looked, and felt, and saw how many teeth they had".

Press accounts conveyed the almost auction-like atmosphere, such as *The Daily Independent of Grand Island, NE,* which in May 1912 reported;

"Some ordered boys, others girls, some preferred light babies, others dark, and the orders were filled out properly and every new parent was delighted."

Babies were easiest to place, but finding homes for children older than 14 was always difficult because of concern that they were too set in their ways or might have bad habits. Children who were physically or mentally disabled or sickly were difficult to find homes for. Although many siblings were sent out together on orphan trains, prospective parents could choose to take a single child, separating siblings. *(Credit: Wikipedia.)*

It should be noted that these children were placed with complete strangers, the majority of whom I'm sure, were good and honest folk who welcomed them into their homes. Nevertheless, these children were taken in by strangers with little or no accountability.

Personally, I would think there's quite a thin line between a noble cause for a child's sake, and free child labour for the sake of the unscrupulous.

There are many disturbing accounts surrounding this relocation scheme of course, and even at the age of 7 or 8 some of the children reported to have no memories prior to arriving at their destination, not even who their parents were. Had they been severely traumatized in their infant years?

In this manner, more than 250,000 orphan children were dispersed throughout the United States between 1854 and 1929 when the program ended.

Around the same time period, Italy was reporting 32,000 foundling children per year, with Spain and Portugal reporting15,000. Before 1860, 374,000 foundling children were processed through the asylum system in Milan, Naples, and Florence alone.

Historian, David L. Ransel reported, that in the 1880's, "Moscow was receiving 16 to 18 thousand infants annually, and sending 10 thousand to outlying villages each year for care." He wrote;

> In 1882 there were all told 41,720 foundlings from the Moscow home living with 32,000 families scattered throughout 4,418 villages. A dozen villages had over 90 fosterings each.

Home Children

During the 1860's the British Government dealt with the surplus of orphans and unwanted children in their own wicked and scandalous way.

'Home Children' was the child migration scheme founded by the infamous Annie MacPherson in 1869, under which more than 100,000 children were forcibly relocated to Canada and New Zealand, but mainly to Australia.

It wasn't unusual for these poor unsuspecting children to be lied to by the authorities, and told that their parent or parents had died.

Deported children were promised a better life in the sun, but instead they got hard labour and life in institutions such as Keaney College in Bindoon, Western Australia. Many were handed over to the Congregation of Christian Brothers, where they were used for hard labour and suffered years of physical and sexual abuse.

This wicked agenda called "home children" was finally exposed one hundred years later by Margaret Humphreys, a social worker from Nottingham. The acclaimed 2010 Australian drama, *Sunshine And Oranges'* is based on her true story.

Australia apologised in 2009 for its involvement in the scheme.

In February 2010, UK Prime Minister Gordon Brown followed suit, and made a formal apology to the families of children who suffered.

Were the British Government sorry for playing their part in causing so much grief for so many families? I very much doubt it.

Just like Boris Johnson and his illegal Lockdown Christmas Parties, they were sorely peeved because they got caught out.

Some researchers estimate that the equivalent of an entire generation of English youth was relocated. Is it possible that the government's justification for their underhand agenda of stealing children, was for the purpose of repopulating certain areas of the Earth?

If so, what happened just as the time period known as 'The Age of Enlightenment' had drawn to a close? Or has the timeline been inverted? Were these disturbing and surrealistic events occurring just as humanity was entering the Dark Age?

For the Industrial Revolution in the Western world, coupled with the ever increasing number of folk suffering from severe mental health issues, and the emerging orphan crisis, ran parallel with other strange phenomena; one of which being, the largely unexplained waves of mass migration.

Strange Phenomena

Beginning in 1815, and running up to the turn of the century, a wave of mass immigration flooded the shores of America. This was due in the main we're told, to famine, civil unrest, religious persecution and war.

Between 1815 and 1860, more than 5 million immigrants arrived in America, mostly from countries like Great Britain, Ireland, Norway, the German states, and Prussia. Between 1845 and 1855 alone, 1.5 million people fled Ireland for the US in the wake of the Potato Famine. This was followed by a huge wave of immigrants flooding in from Italy.

Beginning in the 1850's, large numbers of Asians, including 175,000 Chinese immigrants and 150,000 Japanese immigrants began arriving on American shores. In the years between 1880 and 1900, there was a large acceleration in immigration, with an influx of nearly 9 million people.

In the main, the Europeans especially the Germans, were reasonably secure and self sufficient. But not so with the Irish and Chinese, who typically arrived in America with nothing. This resulted in millions of immigrants taking whatever work was available, usually poorly paid, menial and manual labour.

It's virtually impossible to track down the true number of migrants who who settled in America, Canada, New Zealand and Australia between the years 1851 and 1900, but some researchers estimate the total could be as high as 700 million.

Again, could it be that the true purpose behind this sudden mass migration programme was one of repopulation? Could this have something to do with the virtually empty cities we see in some of the early photographs?

Infantoriums

The as good as unexplained, explosion of folk suffering from mental health issues, the exponential and rapid growth in the number of orphans, along with the millions of folk arriving at the shores of America, was followed by the temporary World Fairs and the permanent Amusement Parks. Both in their own way, a form of escapism from reality.

125

Known as 'the Incubator Doctor', Martin A. Couney, who wasn't a doctor, was best known in medical circles and the public view, for his amusement park sideshow. "The Infantorium" in which visitors paid 25 cents to view premature babies displayed in incubators.

From the late 1800s to the 1930s, permanent Amusement Parks increased in popularity. By 1910, every US city with at least 20,000 people had its own amusement park. Various sources report the existence of between 1,500 and 2,000 amusement parks in the United States by 1919.

Along with ice-cream parlours and hot-dog stalls, sideshows and roller coaster rides, the majority of these fairs had a new and extremely popular attraction. Couney's Infantoriums; the equivalent of today's neonatal intensive care units.

We are told that these fairs provided the only healthcare available for premature babies back in those days. But it's hard to imagine why expectant mothers who went into early labour, would travel to an amusement park, rather than call for the local midwife. In fact, the very notion is hard to make sense of.

With promotional billboards and carnival barkers encouraging folk to part with their money and see "Living Babies", these nurseries were filled with incubators with large glass windows, which for a fee of 25 cents, would allow spectators to view the premature baby inside.

Between 1896 and 1944, a staggering 80,000 premature infants were treated and displayed in amusement parks and fairs, mainly in the United States. Where did such a vast number of premature babies come from? Where were their mothers? Why would people queue up and pay to see infants advertised as 'living babies'? Was it a rare sight to behold at the time? Did the spectators not have their own?

Some people suspect these infantoriums were a front for something else that was going on, something much darker. For exactly what happened to the tens of thousands of premature babies remains somewhat of a mystery. Were they returned to their mothers? Or were they sold or adopted? If something feels disturbingly wrong with the whole premature baby narrative, once again, it's because we have not been told the truth.

Trams

The official history of trams, trolleys or street-cars, began in the early nineteenth century. America's permanent amusement parks were originally known as trolley parks, which were picnic and recreation areas situated along or at the ends of street-car lines.

The information in the following article is adapted from Wikipedia.

The world's first horse-drawn passenger tramway was the Swansea and Mumbles Railway, in Wales, UK, which started operating in 1807. It progressed to steam-driven from 1877, and then, from 1929, by large (106-seater) electric tramcars, until closure in 1961.

The first generation of trams in London started in 1860 when a horse-drawn tramway began operating along Victoria Street in Westminster. But its rail tracks stood proud of the road surface and created an obstruction for other traffic.

Eventually Parliament passed legislation permitting tram services, on the condition that the rails were recessed into the carriageway and that the tramways were shared with other road users. Horse tram lines soon opened all over London, typically using two horses to pull a 60-person car.

From 1885, the North London Tramways Company operated 25 steam engines hauling long-wheelbase trailers, until its liquidation in 1891. Replacement by electric powered vehicles commenced the same year.

The first horse-drawn street-car in America, was the New York and Harlem Railroad's Fourth Avenue Line, which began service in 1832. The first commercial installation of an electric street-car in the United States was in 1884 in Cleveland, Ohio.

This was followed in 1885 by New Orleans, Louisiana, which is the oldest continuously operating street railway system in the world, according to the American Society of Mechanical Engineers. In late 1887 and early 1888, the world's first successful large electric street railway system, was installed in the city of Richmond, Virginia.

A similar pattern is found everywhere, and by the late nineteenth century, tramways were established in most major cities across the realm. Street car networks were gradually retired, as soon as they could be replaced by the more profitable petroleum powered cars and buses.

Yet gifted researcher, Michelle Gibson, shows there is mounting evidence that electric street cars powered by free energy, once existed all over the Earth. Like the old rail tracks which were found

in the middle of the Amazon Forest in Manaus, Brazil, for example.
Originally constructed as a star city named the Fort of São José do
Rio Negro, we are told that it was founded in 1669, and was elevated
to town status in 1832.
From which time, according to the narrative, the early settlers
constructed hundreds of Western European style buildings. These
elaborate structures included a cathedral and a grand opera house
with vast domes, towers, colonnades and gilded balconies, using
glass, crystal and marble imported from Italy. *(Credit:Wikipedia.)*
In other words, old world buildings which were discovered and
inherited by the European settlers in the sixteenth century.
Much like Conquistador Francisco Pizarro perhaps, who in 1543
discovered buildings in Peru, which were equal in grandeur with
European architecture at the time?
Situated 1,500 km up the Amazon River in the middle of the world's
largest rain forest, Manaus was inaccessible by auto-mobile until
1972, and was never reached by railroad. Even when the first main
road to the city was constructed, for much of the year it remained
impassible due to heavy flooding.
Yet Manaus, which was inaccessible by road until 1972, had electric
street lighting and an electric tramway system, 80 years earlier, in
1896?
"An 1895 map shows five tram routes, identified by Roman
numerals. The Viação Suburbana began operation in February 1896
and within a year had 10 passenger coaches and 25 freight cars,
numbered 1-35". *(Credit:tramz.com.)*
To overcome this predicament, the official narrative tells us that the
rubber boom had made possible the electrification of Manaus before
it was installed on many European cities. But the end of the rubber
boom made the generators too expensive to run, and the city was not
able to generate electricity again for years.
Rubber boom or not, personally I find it hard to grasp why tramways
and street lighting would be installed in a virtually inaccessible town
in the middle of the Amazon Rain forest, ahead of many European
cities.
It's not beyond the realm of possibility, that much of the pre-existing
infrastructure across the earth, was inherited by the new elite, the
Robber Barons, who now charged a fee for the provision of

electricity. Likewise, the fast growing reliance on fossil fuels became the source of the fabulous wealth of the elite families.

Some argue that the Industrial Revolution wasn't really a revolution at all, but an applied expansion of pre-existing technology.

Michelle Gibson for example, assumes that all the railroad tracks were just dug up and that all the infrastructure was already in place. She speculates that it was an electrified rail system, and after the free worldwide energy grid was shut down, the free energy sources for mass transportation were replaced by hard to get, oil and coal.

Nothing New Under the Sun

Is it possible that very little, if anything at all, was actually invented or discovered in the 19th and 20th century? Maybe any supposed "new thing" was merely rediscovered, having previously existed *"of old time, which was before us."*

If not in the immediate old world, then maybe the antediluvian world. Perhaps even *"the world that then was"*, back in the generation of the heavens and the earth of old. *(2 Peter 3:4-6.)*

Maybe history repeats itself and only God alone is able to achieve a new thing. For it is written; "There is no new thing under the sun."

The Scriptures inform us that the reason for this is, that things which have already been done, shall yet be achieved again.

Ecclesiastes 1:9. The thing that hath been, it *is that* which shall be; and that which is done *is* that which shall be done: and *there is* no new *thing* under the sun.

Ecclesiastes 1:10. Is there any thing whereof it may be said, See, this is new? it hath been already of old time, which was before us.

Are all the works of man done under the sun merely vanity, as the preacher declared?

Evidence for the existence of a highly advanced civilization in the not too distant past, has been right in front of our faces the whole time. But we fail to see it because we blindly accept the official narrative without question.

Whilst inwardly acknowledging that very little in this world is as it seems.

The Crystal Palace

Conceived in 1849 by Prince Albert, consort of Queen Victoria, and designed by gardener, Sir Joseph Paxton, as a venue for the 1851 London Great Exhibition of all Nations, the Crystal Palace was constructed on an 18 acre site in Hyde Park, London.

The 3-floor structure consisted of an intricate network of cast iron girders, sustaining its walls and a roof of clear glass. Beside the glass, the Palace was supported by 3,300 cast-iron columns and 2,224 principal girders (weighing 9,642 tons) and 24 miles of main gutter; 205 miles of wood sash bar held the glass roof panels in place. *(Folke T. Kihlstedt, Scientific American1984)*.

At three times the size of St. Paul's Cathedral, the final dimensions of the Crystal Palace were 1,848 feet (563 m) long by 456 feet (139 m) wide, and the height of the central transept was 108 feet (33 metres).

The commission in charge of mounting the Great Exhibition was established in January 1850, and it was decided at the outset that the entire project would be funded by public subscription. By 15 March 1850 they were ready to invite submissions, which had to conform to several key specifications: the building had to be *temporary*, simple, as cheap as possible, and economical to build.

On June 11, 1850, Paxton made his original concept drawing, which he doodled with pen and ink onto a sheet of pink blotting paper. This rough sketch (now in the Victoria and Albert Museum) incorporated all the basic features of the finished building.

The Commission finally gave its public endorsement to Paxton's design in July 1850. He now had less than 40 weeks to finalize his plans, manufacture the parts, get them delivered and erect the building in time for the Exhibition's opening, which was scheduled for 1 May, 1851.

Paxton was able to design and build the largest glass structure yet created, from scratch, within ten months, and complete it bang on schedule. (Some sources say nine months, others say eight.)

Complete with an array of interior water features, giant lily pads, trees and a botanical garden, Paxton had created a structure with the greatest area of glass ever seen in a building. It astonished visitors with its clear walls and ceilings that did not require interior lights.

There were over 100,000 exhibits on show, from over 15,000 contributors, stretching for more than ten miles of frontage.

Designed we're told, by glass merchant, Follett Osler, the 27 feet high Crystal Fountain was the world's first glass fountain, made of four tons of pure crystal glass. Programmed to perform with the rich sound of a majestic 4,700-pipe organ, the fountain was displayed in the central court, and was illuminated by electric lights shining up though the columns of water.

'The Art Journal Illustrated Catalogue of the Great Exhibition, London, 1851' *(volume 1, p. 235)* recorded that;

> the fountain was perhaps the most striking object in the exhibition; the lightness and beauty, as well as the perfect novelty of the design, have rendered it the theme of admiration with all visitors. The ingenuity with which this has been effected is very perfect; it is supported by bars of iron, which are so completely embedded in the glass shafts, as to be invisible, and in no degree interfering with the purity and crystalline effect of the whole object

An incredible achievement for a lowly gardener, wouldn't you say? We do have a rough sketch doodled on a piece of pink blotting paper mind, tucked away in a museum. Forgive my sarcasm, but there are so many enigmas and unanswered questions in the official narrative of this *temporary* construction, that just doesn't add up.

How long did it take to level the 800,000 square feet of land the structure was built on? How long did it take to lay all the underground pipework, to construct the water garden and install the plumbing for the 174 submerged fountains?

All we are told is the fantastic story, that the entire building and its water features, were erected in less than 10 months. Even if the Crystal Palace was only a temporary construction, as the official narrative maintains, think how solid the footings would need to be to support an overall weight well in excess of 10 thousand tons.

So why does the narrative claim that no heavy masonry was required for foundations, because the building stood on relatively light concrete footings, which could be left in the ground?

The geometry of the Crystal Palace we're told, was a classic example of the concept of form following manufacturer's limitations: the shape and size of the whole building was directly based around the size of the panes of glass made by the supplier. These were the largest available at the time, measuring 10 inches (25 cm) wide by 49 inches (120cm) long.

Because the entire building was effectively scaled around those dimensions, it meant that nearly the whole outer surface could be glazed using in excess of a million identical panes, thereby drastically reducing both their production cost and the time needed to install them. *[Credit;Wikipedia]*

The 900,000 square feet (84,000 m2) of glass weighing around 400 tons was provided by the Chance Brothers glassworks in Smethwick near Birmingham. At the height of production in January 1851, some 60,000 panes of glass were produced in a fortnight. *[Ref. Hollister P. (1974) The Glazing of the Crystal Palace.]*

And this before the age of automated mass production?

In response to one of Jon Levi's mind-blowing and highly informative YouTube documentaries on the Crystal Palace, one viewer commented;

> Hey there, I'm a commercial Glazier. And the part where you're talking about the amount of glass that was installed by the number of people in the given time frame is physically impossible for a multitude of reasons. Basically each individual Glazier would have to perfectly set and seal 2.678 pieces of glass by themselves every hour for 12 hours a day for 7 days straight with no breaks. This is assuming all 295,000 panes of glass were perfect and fit correctly, none were broken or damaged in transport, and installed without damage correctly on the first attempt. This isn't even possible in the industry today.

The distance from the Smethwick Glassworks to Hyde Park is 134 miles, which even by today's standards is a 2 hour 30 minute journey by road. The only transportation by road in 1851, was the lowly horse and cart or the early steam-driven traction engine, with only steam-powered rail freight or the existing canal system as an alternative option.

Neither Wikipedia nor Encyclopedia Britannica, nor any other source as far as I'm aware, provide any information on exactly how 400 tons of glass and 9,642 tons of cast iron girders were transported all the way to the construction site. A somewhat puzzling matter, wouldn't you say?

Old black and white photographs of the original building in Hyde Park are extremely rare, and virtually impossible to find. This in itself should be enough to challenge the historical record.

The 1851 World Fair in London was the first of its kind, attracting millions of visitors, including royalty, from right across the world. Don't you think both the national and international Press would have been all over it?

The following year, 1852, the Crystal Palace was completely dismantled and relocated to Sydenham Hill (a distance of about 20 miles by road) where it was modified and enlarged. Once again I've not been able to source any information as to how such vast amounts of materials were dismantled and once again slowly transported by horse and cart, to the new construction site.

The new Palace had five rather than three stories, making it half as large again as the original, and nearly twice the height. The area of glass required was now 1,650,000 square feet, such that the glass from the original palace filled less than two-thirds of the need.

Two massive water storage towers were built in the extensive, landscaped grounds, to feed an elaborate system of water-works, including 1,200 fountains, two of which shot water 200 feet into the air. This included the 4-ton Crystal Fountain, plus a more superior pipe-organ, producing an even richer sound for the water to dance to.

The total height of each tower, from the first floor or tier to the top of the chimney cap, was 279 feet, each being 107 feet higher than the Nelson Column in Trafalgar-square. Each tank, when full of water, contained 448,000 imperial gallons, or about 2,000 tons.

Construction we're told, began in 1853 and was completed in 1854. Yet another truly remarkable (or should I say truly impossible) achievement. Like it's predecessor, there are no photographs of the construction process. Do you think it possible the entire story has been fabricated?

An old photograph taken in the 1920s from the top of Sydenham Hill, shows the enormity of the glass structure, and how completely out of character it was, towering high above the rooftops of the brick-built residential buildings around it.

For a number of years the relocated Crystal Palace was the site of shows, exhibitions, concerts, football (soccer) matches, and other entertainments. By the 1890's, the Palace's popularity and state of repair had deteriorated; the appearance of stalls and booths had made it a much more downmarket attraction. Over the next few years the building fell into disrepair, as the huge debt and maintenance costs became unsustainable, and in 1911, bankruptcy was declared. *[Credit Wikipedia].*

On the evening of 30 November 1936, and which still remains an unsolved mystery to this day, an unexplained explosion in a women's wash-room caused an office fire which began to spread quickly and was soon out of control. Although 89 fire engines and over 400 firemen arrived, they were unable to extinguish it. Within hours, the Palace was destroyed and the glow was visible across eight counties. Witnesses described "so much molten glass that it looked like a waterfall"; even "like a Niagara Falls of molten glass."

According to one eyewitness "the glass actually caught fire and when it was really hot there was a sodium flame and the liquid glass was just pouring down." (Ref:Edwards. E. Wincoll, K. (1992) *"The Crystal Palace is on Fire", Memories of the 30th November, 1936.)*

The fire burned most of the night, melting the glass panels and softening the steel superstructure, until one by one, the great supporting arches twisted and fell. By morning, nothing was left but a tangled ruin. In the wake of the fire, most of the remaining metalwork was removed and sold for scrap, and what could not be salvaged was ploughed under, filling in what had been the basement level of the palace.

One-hundred thousand people came to Sydenham Hill to watch the blaze, among them Winston Churchill, who said,

"This is the end of an age".

Maybe truer words were never spoken. An inherited, renovated and repurposed old world structure, on display to the public for one last time before going out in a blaze of glory?

For my guess is, there were actually two of these magnificent glass structures, one located at Hyde Park, the other at Sydenham Hill. Each of these two old world structures, were displayed to the public one last time, before being wantonly destroyed, under the guise of one fabricated narrative.

Yes, I know it sounds crazy. But is the concept any less crazy than the official historical record?

For if the official narrative were to be believed, and cost was not an issue, could an exact copy of this magnificent temporary glass structure be built today? In eight to ten months and by using the same materials? By comparison, roughly the length of time it now takes to build a 4-bedroomed house.

Of course not! Has society forgotten or lost the ability to achieve such a remarkable feat of engineering? Or is it more likely the official narrative is false?

1851 was also the year when the Prime Meridian was re-located to the Royal Observatory at Greenwich, in south-east London. We are spun the fabricated yarn in the mainstream narrative, that the original foundation stone was laid on August 10, 1675, and the original building was completed in the summer of 1676.

The massive old world building, with a tower placed at each of its 4 corners and a central dome, as depicted on a postcard *(c. 1902)* tells a completely different story. It would be impossible to construct such a superb building within a single year today, let alone back in the seventeenth century.

It's very likely that the 1851 Great Exhibition of all Nations, held at the Crystal Palace, marked the beginning of the elite's ongoing venture towards the implementation of their New World Order. The World Fairs that followed were used as a means to showcase the latest inventions in automation, and new forms of technology. And charge a fee for the fossil fuel power source obviously.

The Crystal Palace established an architectural standard for later international fairs and exhibitions that likewise were housed in glass conservatories. The immediate successors being the Cork Exhibition of 1852, the Dublin and New York City expositions of 1853, the Munich Exhibition of 1854, and the Paris Exposition of 1855.

When you look into the history of each of these exhibitions, a similar pattern emerges. Each was held in magnificent old world style buildings which were constructed in record time, and in most cases, were demolished shortly thereafter.

Water Therapy

In 1852, and whilst the relocated Crystal Palace was still under construction, Paxton we're told, was commissioned by Baron Mayer de Rothschild, to design and build the luxurious, Jacobean style, 3-storey country mansion, known as Mentmore Towers in the county of Buckinghamshire. Described as "one of the greatest Victorian houses"in the UK, this beautiful old world structure has a tower on each corner, each topped with antennae.

Construction began on the 60-room building in 1852, and the work we're told, was completed, including the servants quarters, stables and outhouses by 1854. Another impossible task! For once again, this is a fabricated story of a stunning old world building, *inherited* by the Rothschild family, and credited to Joseph Paxton.

Earlier remarkable structures attributed to Joseph Paxton, include the 'Emperor Fountain' and the 'Great Conservatory', built we're told in the mid-nineteenth century in the grounds of Chatsworth House, a stately home set in the picturesque Derbyshire dales, England.

History records how in 1843, William Cavendish, the 6th Duke of Devonshire, decided to construct the world's highest water fountain, and set Joseph Paxton to work to build it.

An eight-acre (348,480 square feet) lake, the Emperor Lake, was dug on the moors 350 feet (110 m) above the house to supply the natural water pressure. The resulting water jet is on record as reaching a height of 296 feet (90 m) or twice the height of 'Nelson's Column'. (*Derby Mercury - Wednesday 28 August 1844.*)

This mammoth project, which necessitated the excavation of over 100,000 cubic yards of earth (approx. 150,000 tons) was completed in just *six* months. (*The Works of Sir Joseph Paxton 1803–1865, George F. Chadwick, 1961, Architectural Press.*)

Around 17,000 tons of soil excavated manually each month for six months straight? Does that even sound feasible to you?

Designed to create a tropical climate for an array of palm trees, water features, aquatic and exotic plants, the Great Conservatory was 275 feet (84m long) 121 feet (37m wide and 62 feet (19m) high, the largest glass building in England at the time.

Inside there was room for two carriages to pass on the main thoroughfare, and a flight of stairs, hidden by ascending rocks, led to a gallery from which one could inspect the highest branches of the exotic palms and other trees flourishing there. Here Paxton grew bananas and pineapples, and giant tropical lily pads, sturdy enough to support a young child.

To create this climate there were eight underground boilers fuelled by coal, which arrived by underground rail wagons. The boilers fed a seven-mile maze of 6-inch hot water pipes.

Allegedly completed in 1840, the Great Conservatory was quite a remarkable achievement for a time before the birth of the first modern power tool, wouldn't you say? Yet again there are obvious and major flaws, both in the official narrative and the given timeline. Do you think it possible there's something the 'controllers' of history don't want us to know? Or do they really think we're that gullible? The magnificent Great Conservatory was demolished in 1920, leaving only the supporting walls as a lasting memorial to this extraordinary building. Another act of wanton destruction.

In one of his brilliant documentaries, Ewaranon records how in 2018 there was a heatwave in England, and viewed from the air, the former glory of the Chatsworth estate started appearing in the grounds themselves. The faint footprints of old buildings that no longer exist, and visual evidence that the entire estate was once a massive farm.

The Chatsworth Estate and the River Derwent that flows through it was once a vast area of farmland, and the main building most likely used to accommodate the workers. With its tumbling water features, fountains, streams and cascades, the Chatsworth Estate it seems, was originally part of the worldwide electromagnetic energy grid serving the British Isles.

Palaces, stately homes and mansions, were never constructed to house the elite, they were originally the central hub of the massive farms of old. The farms themselves were likely cultivated with sound, vibrational frequencies and energized water, which was used to encourage growth and to cultivate the farm produce.

Even contemporary scientists acknowledge that sound waves, frequencies and electro-magnetic ionized particles in the atmosphere strongly influence the growth of fruit and vegetables. In 1902, Karl Selim Lemström, a Finnish geophysicist, discovered that the trees under the Aurora Borealis grew faster than the same trees under different conditions. Most of the earlier electro-magnetic experiments failed however, as the experimental conditions varied from one location to another. Any variation in the wide range of the natural elements could lead to a very different outcome.

The huge outbuilding at Chatsworth which in all likelihood once housed the generator, has since been repurposed as luxurious stables. Atop of the hill next to the Emperor Lake stands a large quadruple capacitor, or water storage tower, which was repurposed as a hunting tower. The central engine which has since been removed, was likely set in the octagonal stone structure located in the grounds. This has been repurposed as a larder, to store the hunted game.

Who was this super achiever, and did he even exist? Or was Paxton hand-picked by the controllers to play the leading role in a partially fictitious story, to explain away impossible structures that shouldn't exist at the time?

In 1951 the Peak District was designated as a National Park. There are reservoirs, rivers, waterways and various old world structures everywhere, many of which are mansions or stately homes etc. But the inhabitants of the Peak District did not build all this glorious infrastructure in the nineteenth century, they inherited it.

The abundance of stately homes, mansions and manors, all point to the massive farming practices of the old world. Like Chatsworth and the Crystal Palace, the controllers of the narrative had to ensure these building could never be used again for their original, intended purposes, nor for any of the inheritors to discover their true function.

The Peak District is home to two large towns, Matlock, which is renowned for its historical baths, and Buxton is famed for its bottled water. Both towns boast quite a collection of old world structures.

In the 1850's, Matlock began its spectacular growth as a Spa Town, and in 1856, local businessman John Smedley, established Smedley's Hydro and its water tower, which is now a Government council building. Smedley's Hydro was the first hydropathic hotel, and in its heyday, was the largest of the 20 or so hydropathy's that opened in the region.

With the use of natural, or spa water, the hydropathy's were able to handle hundreds of patients, and at the time were tremendously successful in curing a whole range of illnesses and complaints, as well as having a therapeutic impact on mental health patients.

Electric bells were installed throughout the building, and natural or spa water was used for curing disease, along with sound, frequency, vibration and electricity. Such treatments included electric therapy, ultraviolet rays and diathermy. Rather than a heat source, diathermy uses energy sources like sound and electricity, which are converted into heat by the human body.

Smedley was able to heat the entire building with a water heating system built into its walls, which maintained a constant temperature of 65 degrees, even when the establishment was filled with a crowd of 200 or more visitors. How did they have the ability to do this in the nineteenth century? It seems that Smedley used energized water to achieve this remarkable feat.

Over the years, Smedley had many run-ins with local and national newspaper reporters and the medical establishment, who invariably portrayed the practice of hydropathy as being pseudoscience.

In the late twentieth century, a number of hydro-pathic institutions wholly transferred their operations away from therapeutic purposes to become tourist hotels, whilst still retaining the name 'Hydro'. All of its health benefits through the use of sound, frequency and vibration have been eradicated.

Hydropathy today is seen as little more than a relaxing bath venture, and all of its original use of vibrational energy and electricity are a thing of the past. Most folk now associate a 'spa break' with a weekend of relaxation, a massage or two, a dip in the pool, and cosmetic or beauty treatment.

Smedley's mission, it would seem, was to carefully control the introduction of Hydropathy, for a limited time, for the end purpose of declaring it fraudulent and quackery, and completely dismiss it is as a serious practise. Much like Nikola Tesla, Smedley introduced and demonstrated the science of the old world for a limited time, only to have it debunked, side-lined, and banished for ever.

The history books were now able to justify the entire waterway system of the Peak District, successfully preventing subsequent generations from questioning its presence. Yet, when one becomes aware of what they're actually looking at, the remains of the former energy grid and water system are evident all across the UK.

War of the Currents

Starting in the late 1880s, Thomas Edison and Nikola Tesla were embroiled in a battle now known as the "War of the Currents".

Tesla defended the holistic model of the old world, thinking in terms of energy, frequencies and vibration, and did not want the new world of energy production to end up in the hands of a few.

Edison developed (or actually redeveloped) direct current (DC) that runs continually in a single direction, like in a battery or a fuel cell, which during the early years of electricity, was the standard in both the UK and the US.

But there was one problem. Direct current is not easily converted to higher or lower voltages.

Tesla believed that alternating current (or AC) was the solution to this problem. Alternating current reverses direction a certain number of times per second, and can be converted to different voltages relatively easily using a transformer.

The Chicago World's Fair also known as the World's Columbian Exposition, took place in 1893, at the height of the Current War.

General Electric bid to electrify the fair using Edison's direct current for $554,000, but lost to George Westinghouse, who said he could power the fair for only $399,000 using Tesla's alternating current.

Westinghouse Electric had severely underbid the contract and struggled to supply all the equipment specified, including twelve 1,000 horsepower single phase AC generators and all the lighting and other equipment required. to decorate the buildings with incandescent lights, illuminate fountains, and power three huge spotlights.

Westinghouse also won the major part of the contract to build the Niagara Falls hydroelectric project later that year *(Credit: Wikipedia)*

D.C. commercial power distribution systems declined rapidly in numbers throughout the 20th century, but the last DC system in New York City was shut down in 2007.

Today our electricity is still predominantly powered by alternating current, but computers, LEDs, solar cells and electric vehicles all run on DC power.

Some available information suggests that after the worldwide, game-changing event, which many refer to as the Mud Flood, there remained countless areas of land, complete with many huge and beautiful structures, especially in America. These buildings, which once served an entirely different purpose, were inherited by the new power elite, aka the Robber Barons, which they then subsequently repurposed as "World's Fairs".

The mysterious World Expositions, or World Fairs, were a means to showcase the latest advances in technology to the general public, and to transition them into the modern era of electricity, which was dominated by the use of Alternating Current.

During the transition stage, it's extremely likely, that some of the old world technology was still being used before it was phased out. Evidence for this can be seen in some of the old photographs and film footage of the 1901 Pan-American Exposition held on a 350-acre site at Buffalo, New York, which were taken at night.

The buildings themselves were majestic, and almost appear to be luminescent, and show illuminated towers and structures on a scale, which has never been seen again to this day. They were lit up with an incredible brightness, making the powerful lanterns standing next to them pale by comparison.

Some suggest that the central 411 foot Electric Tower was lit up by half a million light bulbs. It must have been an absolutely mind-blowing experience for the hundreds of thousands of people who had previously only seen gas light or candle light.

Example below is a screenshot taken from Ewaranon's 'Lost History of the Flat Earth'.

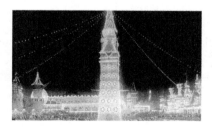

Other stunning photographs show the entire area bathed in a golden glow, with coloured beams of light criss-crossing and illuminating the night sky. Old world technology at its finest, and never to be seen again.

We are told by Wikipedia that;

"the advent of the alternating current power transmission system in the US allowed designers to light the Exposition in Buffalo using power generated 25 miles (40km) away at Niagara Falls."

Yet nobody has ever explained how Tesla, or anyone else for that matter, managed to achieve such a remarkable feat. We are left with little option but to second guess.

There is much to suspect that the Robber Barons hijacked many of the old world architectural wonders, in which some of the former technology was contained.

Is it possible that a superior form of technology was used to electrify the 1901 Pan-American Exposition? Could this be why we have never witnessed such an awesome display of electrical illumination since?

Like all of the world fairs, we are told that by far the majority of the buildings at the Pan-American Exposition, were erected purely on a temporary basis, and were constructed of timber and steel framing with precast staff panels made of a plaster and fibre mix.

However, and like all the World Fairs, the attention to detail was so great, that purely visually there seems to be no difference whatsoever between the Exposition buildings and the splendour of the classical buildings of antiquity.

Of the Palace of Fine Arts for example, Professor van Noppen of Columbia University noted that;

> The Palace of Fine Arts is so sublime, so majestic, and is the product of such imagination that it would have graced the age of Pericles."

With equal enthusiasm, Thomas Edison said;

> The architect of that building is a genius. There is nothing equal anywhere on earth.

It's not easy to imagine that these two eyewitnesses were talking about a brand new building, made from the simplest and cheapest of materials, and one merely constructed on a temporary basis.

Demolition of the buildings began in March 1902, and within a year, most of the buildings were destroyed.

It's very likely that the 1851 Great Exhibition of all Nations, held at the Crystal Palace, London, marked the beginning of the controllers transition period from the old world into the modern day era.

It's alleged that one third of the population of Britain, around six million people, paid homage to the Crystal Palace.

Western Europe, Australia, New Zealand and America, which were mostly controlled by the Cabal at the time, hosted virtually all of the world's fairs. The world expositions of 1851 London, 1853 New York, 1862 London, 1876 Philadelphia, 1889 Paris, 1893 Chicago, 1897 Brussels, 1900 Paris, 1901 Buffalo, 1904 St. Louis, 1915 San Francisco, and 1933–34 Chicago, were landmarks in this respect.

Each of these fairs consisted of hundreds of truly remarkable buildings, many of which were colossal.

Furthermore, the majority of these buildings, which we are told were only intended to be *temporary*, were constructed in record time, and were demolished soon after completion.

The prize for the speediest quick-build without a doubt, has to go to those who designed and constructed the Hotel Internacional for the 1888 Barcelona World Fair.

Built on 5,000 square metres (54,000sqft) of reclaimed land, the hotel stood five stories tall at 150 by 35 metres (492ft ×115ft). Its capacity was for 2,000 guests in 600 rooms and 30 apartments for large families. According to the official narrative, this luxurious hotel was built in a mere *69 days* from the middle of December 1887 to February 14, 1888. The coldest and darkest weeks of the year.

An impossible task, for which there can only be two possible explanations. *1*: If constructed in the 1880s as we are told, the builders had far more advanced technology and forms of transport than we are aware of.

2: It was originally an old world structure which had been inherited by the controllers, and was merely renovated in a record 69 days, and completed just in time for the Barcelona World Fair.

According to Wikipedia, because right from the outset this huge 630 room building, was only intended to serve a temporary purpose, it was designed and erected without any foundations as such. Instead, it rested on a metal framework to give it stability. If that doesn't seem plausible to you, again it's because we are not being told the truth.

Again, old photographs of the Hotel Internacional, show people dressed in a style one would expect to see in the Victorian era, yet without the means and ability to construct the huge and impressive architecture around them. Or certainly not within a period of less than six months.

The demolition process began on May 1, 1889, just over a year since its inauguration.

A Clear Statement

The Luciferian controllers of this realm have a tendency to declare their intent to the public beforehand, often by 'hiding' things in plain sight. If the public fail to see it, the onus rests upon the public. Not with the controllers, who declared their intent for all to see beforehand. In fact, they believe they are legally bound to do so, by God Himself.

The word "exposition", has two given meanings in the Dictionary, the first being;

"A statement that explains something clearly."

Hence, the World Expositions gave the controllers of the narrative, a final opportunity to openly and clearly showcase to the public, many of the grand buildings and technological wonders of the old world, before they were deliberately destroyed and hidden away forever.

They destroyed thousands of them, with maybe a few left standing, that still serve some kind of purpose. The same is true with all the Expositions, Exhibitions and World Fairs for at least 100 years, between 1851 and the 1950's.

Officially, the purpose of the World Fairs, was to make the public aware of the supposedly "new" technologies born out of the Industrial Revolution, and to create new markets for commerce. Yet the more carefully one investigates, the more difficult it becomes to find plausible and logical explanations for the construction and destruction of these extraordinary and huge exhibition areas.

One can only conclude that there was a hidden agenda behind all of this strangeness, and that we have not been told the truth.

Was there something to hide? If so, what?

World Fairs

Following the end of the American Civil War, Americans began to prepare for the celebration of the nation's 100th birthday in 1876. The Centennial International Exhibition of 1876, the first official World's Fair to be held in the US, was held in Philadelphia, Pennsylvania, for a period of six months, from May 10 to November 10, 1876.

At a cost of more than $11 million, the fair was a complete financial failure. Many of these expositions were a financial disaster, and as one researcher into the mystery of the world fairs noted;

> Quite a few Fairs were enormous monetary losses. This is astonishing in that the initial motivation for the exhibitions supposedly came from the industrialists themselves. The investment deficits could indicate that the Fairs had a hidden agenda that was not profit-oriented.

The 450 acre Fairmount Park in which the 1876 Exhibition was held, was enclosed within a 9 feet high wood-panel fence which ran for nearly three miles. In the midst of water features, lagoons and canals, the footpaths and drives within the grounds stretched for seven miles, while five and a half miles of narrow-gauge steam operated rail-way, surrounded and intersected them.

More than 200 buildings were constructed within the Exposition's grounds, of which the organizers said;

"The general verdict of all who saw them is that they were faultless in design and perfect in construction". *(City of Philadelphia, Records Department, City Archives, RG 230.)*

Then one by one the buildings, both large and small that dotted the landscape disappeared. The majority of the smaller buildings, were in all likelihood ***not*** built to last, being constructed using a wooden framework, complimented with bricks, concrete and plaster.

Not so with the massive, glorious and totally breath-taking main buildings. There were five main buildings in the exposition, the largest being the alleged ***temporary*** structure, the Main Exhibition Building. At the time it was the largest building in the world by area, enclosing 21.5 acres. It measured 464 feet in width and 1,880feet in length. *(Philadelphia: A 300-Year History, p. 462.)*

Yet while it's claimed this amazing building was only erected as a *temporary* structure, according to Wikipedia;

> The flooring of the building was made of wooden planks
> that rested directly on the ground without any air space
> underneath them.

Seriously? No solid foundations? Just thousands of wooden planks
laid out on the ground? Please bear this absurd claim in mind as you
check out this 1878 engraving of the Main Exhibition Building
(from Earl Shinn, Walter Smith & Joseph M. *Wilson.)*

It was constructed, or so we're told, using prefabricated parts with a
wood and iron frame resting on a substructure of 672 stone piers.
Wrought iron roof trusses were supported by the columns of the
superstructure.

Columns were placed at a uniform distance of 24 feet and the entire
structure consisted of 672 columns, the shortest column being 23feet
in length and the longest 125feet in length.

The structure of the building featured a central avenue with a series
of parallel sheds that were 120 feet wide, 1,832 feet long, and 75
feet high. On both sides of the nave were avenues 100 feet in width
and 1,832 feet in length. Aisles 48 feet wide were located between
the nave and the side avenues, and smaller aisles 24 feet in width
were on the outer sides of the building.

The exterior of the building featured four towers, each being 75 feet
high, at each of the building's corners. Each tower had small
balconies set at different heights that served as observation galleries.
(Credit:Wikipedia.)

Can you even begin to imagine the overall weight of this colossal
building, and the sheer volume of stress endured by the wooden
planks supporting it? Does it even sound feasible? Furthermore, we
are told the entire building took just eighteen months to complete.

This is obviously not the case, for when you study the available pictures, there appears to be nothing "temporary" whatsoever about this beautiful, oversized building. One is left with little doubt that whoever built it, it was built to last, maybe even for centuries.

Even if such were the case, it would be an impossible feat to construct this massive building, even on a temporary basis within a mere 18 months.

Nevertheless, five years later, the building was demolished in 1881.

The other main buildings were equally impressive, each in its own way. The Machinery Hall was the second largest structure, which in this case, didn't rely on thousands of wooden planks to support it. Rather, it rested on a foundation of massive masonry.

With a superstructure made of wood and glass (so we're told) the main hall was 1,402 feet long and 360 feet wide, with a wing of 208 feet by 210 feet attached on the south side of the building. The length of the building was 18 times its height, and with eight separate entrances, it occupied 558,440 square feet (12.8 acres).

In the next breath, we're told this huge and impressive building took a mere *six* months to construct. Unbelievable!

The Machinery Hall was demolished the following year in 1877. Hardly surprising I guess, considering it only took *six* months to construct.

According to Wikipedia, the third-largest structure at the exposition was the Agricultural Hall. The building was 820 feet long and 540 feet wide. Made of wood and glass, the structure was designed to look like various barn structures pieced together. This short description however, doesn't do any justice whatsoever, to the impressive neo-Gothic architecture of the building we see in the photos and sketches.

Rather than being made of wood and glass, as the official narrative states, every image or painting I've come across, indicates this vast building with its 10 individual towers, was largely constructed with brick and stone.

Thus far, and having checked multiple sources, I've been unable to find the date when this magnificent structure was demolished.

The Horticultural Hall, which was designed in the Moorish style, had an iron and glass frame on a brick and marble foundation and was 193 feet long, 38 feet wide and 68feet tall.

Unlike the other main buildings, we're told the massive Horticultural Hall was meant to be permanent.

Was it merely a coincidence that after the Exposition had ended, the **only** main building which was meant to be **permanent**, fell into disrepair and was closed down?

Yes, I guess so, but only if you believe in coincidence.

In 1954, the building was severely damaged by Hurricane Hazel, and was subsequently demolished. *(The Philadelphia Inquirer, January 18, 2022.)*

Now, what do they say about an ill wind?

Of all the exhibition's main buildings, the jewel in the crown was the Art Gallery Building, now known as the Memorial Hall, and is one of only two of the original 200 buildings which was not torn down. The other being the traditional-style Swedish Cottage, which was later re-erected in Central Park, New York.

Built on a massive 1.5-acre site, the Memorial Hall was constructed with brick, glass, iron, and granite in the beaux-arts style, with a 150-foot dome atop a 59-foot-high structure. The central domed area is surrounded by four elegant pavilions on the corners, with open arcades to the east and west of the main entrance.

After the exposition, the Memorial Hall reopened in 1877 as the Pennsylvania Museum of Art.

One final thought; over the six months the fair was open to the public, it was attended by nearly 10 million people, according to organizers. That amounts to well in excess of 1.5 million visitors per month, or roughly 375,000 visitors per week.

Personally, I find it hard to believe that in 1876 (ten years before the first motorized vehicle) one million more people travelled to this exhibition than the approximate nine million folk who visit Disney Land, California, in a six month period today.

Especially when taking into account our modern-day network of fast travel motorways, high speed train service, and regular internal and international air-flights.

I'm not suggesting the Centennial Exhibition didn't take place, but like all the World Fairs, there remains an air of mystery surrounding it, for there is so much that makes little sense.

Why spend millions of dollars erecting these excessive, resplendent buildings if only to destroy them a few years later? I encourage everyone to check out the images of these magnificent structures, for there doesn't appear to be anything temporary about them. On the contrary, they seem to be built to last, and even the organizers said; *"The general verdict of all who saw them is that they were faultless in design and perfect in construction"*.

When taking a closer look at some of the photos of supposedly brand new buildings however, some of them seem to show the process of ageing and weather erosion. Certainly not what one would expect to see in a brand new structure. For if the official story is coherent, temporary or not, shouldn't all of these buildings have looked brand new?

I suspect the majority of these buildings already existed, but were located on privately owned land, which was cordoned off, but later opened to the public, and utilized to host the grand, no expense spared, World Fairs.

Hard to get one's head around, but once again such lavish extravagance, followed by wanton acts of destruction suggests a certain group of people had an agenda, or reason for doing so. Yet another case of restoring these marvellous structures which were left behind by the unknown builders.

Once completely renovated, they were used to showcase the new advances in manufacturing, science, art and technology to the public as part of the transition into the new world.

Having served their purpose, and put on display to a gullible public for one last time, one by one, these magnificent old world structures were demolished.

• Writes American art historian, Russel Lynes in his 1954 book, *'The Tastemakers';*

> Critics today look back upon the Centennial Exhibition as an architectural and artistic calamity that produced not a single new idea but was, rather, the epitome of accumulated bad taste of the era that was called the Gilded Age, the Tragic Era, the Dreadful Decade, or the Pragmatic Acquiescence, depending on which epithet you thought most searing.

The highly elaborate, extravagant and supposedly *temporary* lobbies palaces, pavilions, statues, halls, water features and other facades built during a time of economic depression for the late nineteenth century and early twentieth century World's Fairs raises serious questions. In fact, the very statement "temporary building" being attached to these buildings should set an alarm bell ringing.

Why build them in the first place, if only to demolish them at a later date? Or did they already exist as old world structures, and were merely renovated to serve a temporary purpose?

Once completed, let's say a final goodbye to yet another trace of the old world?

The very notion that anyone in the western world with half a brain, would erect such a large number of *temporary* Greco-Roman style complexes, majestically adorned with fluted, 'fake' marble columns, vaulted roofs complete with antennae, towers, buttresses, ornate fake-gold domes, and display them to the public for a limited time before tearing them down, just doesn't sit right somehow.

Each structure we're told, consisted of a wooden framework which was covered and bulked out with cement, plaster of Paris, jute fibre and straw, as was allegedly the case with the 200 plus, temporary buildings at the 1893 Columbian Exposition, aka the World's Fair in Chicago.

Photographs of these supposedly temporary buildings raise a number of questions. Especially when having served their purpose, these magnificent structures were greeted by the giant wrecking ball.

Below is a screenshot from Lost History of the Flat Earth, of the Administration Building and Grand Court. Does it look like a temporary building with a wooden framework, disguised with a lick of white paint and other structural cosmetics to you?

The White City

Erected so we're told, upon 690 acres of reclaimed swampland and dubbed the 'White City', visitors at the Chicago World Fair were not permitted to take personal snapshots and very few photographs of its actual construction can be found. In a number of cases it could even be argued that many of these were actually end of life photographs, which were taken during the demolition process, rather than during their construction.

There were fourteen main "great buildings", each centred around a series of tumbling cascades, water fountains, and a giant reflective pool called the Grand Basin. An official collection of stunning photographs revealing their grandeur can be found on the Internet, which were taken before the White City was demolished within just a few decades of its construction.

I've never worked in the construction industry, but temporary or not, good old fashioned common sense tells me that structures this size require huge foundations, especially when erected right next to the water. It appears there is no consistent or reliable information answering such questions in any of the literature.

The Manufacturer's and Liberal Arts Building for example, was the largest of the Chicago Word Fair's great buildings.

At 1,687 feet long and 787 feet wide, it required twice as much steel as the Brooklyn Bridge. The building's total floor space was the equivalent of 23 football fields and contained over 44 acres of exhibit space.

The height of the roof truss over the central line was two hundred and twelve feet nine inches, and its span three hundred and fifty-four feet in the clear. *(Credit: Wikipedia.)*

The following year, on January 8, 1894, the Manufactures and Liberal Arts buildings along with the magnificent Peristyle and Quadriga burned to the ground, leaving only the twisted, underlying framework.

High up on the pedestal supporting the Quadriga was the Biblical inscription, the word of Jesus;

Ye Shall Know the Truth, and the Truth Shall Make You Free.

The 'truth' according to the official narrative that we're expected to believe without question however, is far more likely to bring bondage than freedom. In which case, only by asking the right questions can freedom be attained. For knowledge begins with asking questions, especially the right ones.

The Louisiana Purchase Exposition 1904

From April 30 to December 1, 1904, the St. Louis World's Fair was held on a 1,200-acre site, and was the largest fair (in area) to date. The Exposition boasted of over 1,500 buildings, connected by some 75 miles of roads and walkways.

The vast Palace of Agriculture alone covered some 20 acres. It was said to be impossible to give even a hurried glance at everything in less than a week.

Wikipedia inform us that:

> One of the most popular attractions of the Exposition was contained in the Palace of Transportation: automobiles and motor cars. The automobile display contained 140 models including ones powered by gasoline, steam, and electricity. The private automobile first made its public debut at the Louisiana Purchase Exposition. Four years after the Louisiana Purchase Exposition, the Ford Motor Company began producing the Ford Model T making the personal automobile more affordable.

As with the World's Columbian Exposition in Chicago in 1893, we're told that *all* but *one* of the St. Louis World Fair's grand, neoclassical exhibition palaces, were *temporary* structures, designed to last but a year or two. They were built, so we're told, with a material called "staff," a mixture of plaster of Paris and hemp fibres, on a wooden framework.

I haven't a clue as to how they achieved such ornate detail by using plaster of Paris and hemp, which, by the way, would be very porous and absorb any water it came into contact with. A good down pour or two would cause the plaster to dissolve.

Once again, when looking through the available photographs, there just doesn't appear to be anything temporary about them. In fact it was not just the glorious structures above ground. A number of the buildings had a network of underground waterways.

The massive Creation Hall for example, where "fairgoers travelled by boat through a labyrinth of underground passages to a roomy cavern, where they were diverted by illusions in the form of living heads that have no bodies to support them." *(St. Louis Public Library Digital Collections.)*

Why anyone would want to invest so much time, effort and money into building a temporary underground waterway system, is hard to fathom. Likewise, who in their right mind would build basements under the ground for a temporary exhibition? No wonder photos are hard to come by.

The existence of these huge buildings of such finery and grandeur is not in dispute. The question is, who built them? And when?

Were these buildings, which we are told were erected on a temporary basis, actually permanent old world structures, which had been inherited by the controllers?

Photographs of various buildings surrounded by scaffolding, and supposedly under construction, are not actual evidence for construction. For they could equally have been taken as the buildings were being refurbished, or even during the final demolition process. Apart from this, how was it possible to construct 1500 buildings and prepare over 75 miles of road, in approximately two and a half years?Only to be destroyed 9 months later.

After the fair closed, nearly all of its structures were demolished within a short time, leaving only a few footprints, ponds, and canals in Forest Park in St. Louis.

It appears that the Expo 'organizers' plan always was to completely destroy everything after the exhibitions ended. However this often resulted in a public outcry, meaning that at least some of these structures were preserved.

A word to the wise

Bearing in mind that the primary meaning of the word Exposition is; *"A statement that explains something clearly,"*maybe Helen Keller tried to convey a message; a word to the wise.

For the author and disability rights activist gave a lecture in the main auditorium at the St. Louis World Fair, in which she said;

"People do not like to think. If one thinks, one must reach conclusions. Conclusions are not always pleasant."

For when folk actually do take the time to stop to think, there is really only one conclusion. All that we see and all that we're told about these world fairs is an elaborate impossibility. It's all utter nonsense.

Don't be fobbed off by those who say "trust the science and those in authority and don't ask questions."

Look where that's got us today. The world we currently live in, is a direct result of these mysterious world expositions. For the World Fairs held in the mid nineteenth century were essentially a period of transition into the age of Alternating Current and the internal combustion engine, both controlled by the new elite aka the Robber

Barons.

A classic example of this and quite an eye opener, can be seen in the early black and white films on YouTube such as; "A Trip Through Paris in the late 1890s".

Against a backdrop of magnificent architecture we see pedestrians, bicycles, the horse and carriage, the horse-drawn fire engine, and the early motorized vehicle. Then lo and behold; we see the less energetic pedestrians taking life easy, as they hop aboard to join the crowd being carried along by the electric powered, moving pavement. The transition phase from the old world into the modern-day era, caught on celluloid film. This is emphasized by the massive, and regal old world buildings, towering high in the background.

In fact, we see a society largely dominated by Christian ethics, but without the ability to construct these huge and magnificent buildings surrounding them. Like most of the earliest black and white footage of cities, at times it appears these people were picking up, from where a previous people left off.

Far more could be written about the World Fairs, and all the other strange goings on during the nineteenth and early twentieth century. But hopefully I've covered enough to encourage you the reader, to pause for a while, and think. Especially if you have never considered the hidden history aspect of the world that we live in.

Having considered in part, just how much of world history has been manipulated by the controllers, it's time to ask serious questions. For it would almost seem that the controllers don't want us to know about certain events of the past. Nor the actual age we reside in.

Writes former Czech exile, Milan Kundera, on the back cover of *The Book of Laughter and Forgetting* (May, 1996.)

> The first step in liquidating a people is to erase its memory. Destroy its books, its culture, its history. Then have someone write new books, manufacture a new culture, invent a new history. Before long the nation will begin to forget what it is and what it was.

Faith versus Religion

The Authorized King James Bible is more accurate than most people understand. It is man and his religious ideals and practises who bring its teachings into question, and often into disrepute.

Jesus taught "not to kill", to "love God with all your heart and soul". *(Matthew 22:37)* and how a pure and undefiled religion in the eyes of God, is to care for the orphans and widows who are suffering, and not to become embroiled in the affairs of this world. *(James 1:27.)*

He also condemned the hypocrisy of those who were under the illusion that they could make themselves righteous through keeping the Law of Moses, by performing ritualistic practises, and by adopting the religious traditions of man.

"Worship the Father in spirit and in truth", Jesus told them. *(John 4:23.)*

In other words, Jesus keeps things relatively simple, whereas man, often influenced by the enemy of souls, has a tendency to complicate things.

2 Corinthians 11:3. But I fear, lest by any means, as the serpent beguiled Eve through his subtilty, so your minds should be corrupted from the simplicity that is in Christ.

Jesus sent his apostles out to *teach* the nations, *not* to make them Christians. The disciples and the early followers of Jesus, *never* used the word 'Christian' to describe themselves.

The term was first used in a derogatory sense by the secular population of Rome, who used the word to ridicule followers of Jesus, those who were willing to suffer persecution on His behalf. Hence why 1 Peter 4:16 states;

"Yet if any man suffer as a Christian, let him not be ashamed; but let him glorify God on this behalf".

Yet over the centuries the term 'Christian' has become associated with most all nations and civilizations of the western world.

Genuine Christians are imperfect folk, who have their own personal inner battles, usually on a daily basis. What unites Christians worldwide, is not the "church" they attend, nor the "denomination" they belong to. The one thing that unites them is their own personal faith in Jesus, which at the same time is a faith shared by all other true Christians across the entire realm, regardless of generation, of race or nationality.

All share the same genuine belief that their only hope of salvation unto eternal life, rests entirely upon the grace of God, through faith in his Son, the Lord Jesus Christ, who shed his blood on the tree for the redemption of sin. For Jesus is the Lamb of God which taketh away the sin of the world *(John 1:29)* by the sacrifice of himself. *(Hebrews 9:26)*.

Yet although God so loved the world, Jesus prayed NOT for the world, but rather, for all those chosen in Him before this world/age began *(Ephesians 1:4)*. Those which belong to the Father. *(John 17:9)*. and given to Jesus, whom he then purchased with his own blood *(Acts 20:28)* before he returned to the Father.

A Christian by name only (nominal) may well be a regular church attendee, or member of a church choir etc. but has been described as "a person who has not responded in repentance and faith to Jesus Christ as his personal Saviour and Lord".

Furthermore, many who do not even believe the Bible to be true, presume to teach it.

This is why Billy Graham for example, could call himself a Christian, whilst also being an oath-sworn 33 degree Luciferian Free Mason. And why in 1991, George Bush Sr. casually referred to the mass slaughter of 6,000 Iraqis on the 'Highway of Death' as they were retreating from Kuwait, as a "Turkey Shoot."

How on earth can 'do not kill', 'love God' and 'love your neighbour' be so difficult to understand?

Both George Bush Junior and Senior are generally recognized as Christians yet at the same time are oath-sworn Skull & Bones, and Bohemian Grove Satanists.

Unlike the teachings of man (i.e. traditional religious belief systems and *inherited* theology), Faith itself, can *not* be *inherited*. Faith is a gift which comes by hearing the word of God. *(Romans 10:17.)*

Personal faith is not a blind faith as some suppose, but an active and a thoughtful one.

To quote the words of eighteenth century English theologian, John Hutchinson;

"Unthinking Faith is a curious offering to be made to the Creator of the Human Mind".

Eschatology

Over the years since coming to faith in the Lord Jesus Christ, I've always shared the commonly held view, that essentially follows an ongoing fulfillment of prophecy which starts in Daniel's time (circa 530 B.C.) and continues down the ages through John's writing of the Book of Revelation all the way to the second coming of Jesus Christ. From such a perspective, the majority of the prophetic events recorded in the New Tesament, especially in Revelations, are still future, as I was originally taught.

Furthermore, I was taught that the *"time, times and an half"* in Daniel 12:7 refers to the final 3.5 years, 42 months or 1,260 days of great tribulation prior to His return.

From a historicist view, the "time, times, and an half" relates to 3 1/2 years, 42 months or 1, 260 days, which corresponds exactly with the worst tribulation in Jewish history. This began in 66 A.D. with three major rebellions by the Jews against the Roman Empire. Many early Chstians believed that Nero's persecution of Christians in 64–65 AD was the chaos preceding the advent of the messianic age.

Revelation 13:5. And there was given unto him a mouth speaking great things and blasphemies; and power was given unto him to continue *forty and two months*.

It's a historical fact that Nero began to persecute the Christians throughout the Roman Empire around mid-November 64 AD. This intense persecution only ended when Nero committed suicide in June 68 AD. Thus he made war on the saints for a period of exactly *42 months*.

The saints were called to endure and remain faithful, in light of the fact that the beast who so often wielded the sword, would himself be killed by the sword. *(Revelation 13:10, 14).*

In June 68 AD Nero ended his life by thrusting his sword through his own throat, with the help of his personal secretary, Epaphroditus, in part because he realized that his popularity had waned, and also because of an attempted coup. Nero lived by the sword, and died by the sword.

Tertullian [145-220 AD] credited "Nero's cruel sword" as providing the martyr's blood as seed for the church. At one point he urged his readers to "consult your histories; you will find there that Nero was

157

the first who assailed with the imperial sword the Christian sect."

The beast from the sea would be given much support from a second beast (from the earth), which would compel "the earth and its inhabitants" to worship the first beast. An image of the first beast would be given breath, so that it might "even speak and might cause those who would not worship the image of the beast to be slain" *(Revelation 13:11-15).*

The late first century pseudepigraphical Judaeo-Christian text, the so-called 'Testament of Hezekiah', contains the concept that at the end of the world, Belial, aka the Antichrist will manifest himself as the reincarnation of the dead Nero. The text predicts that the great angel "will descend from his firmament in the form of a man, a king of iniquity". He will come with all power, and will say, "I am the Lord, and before me there was no one. And all men in the world will believe in him." *(IV.1-8).*

Paul Kroll (1999), of Grace Communion International, notes that early church writers Justin Martyr and Irenaeus (among others) wrote of Simon Magus (mentioned in Acts 8:9-24) as being able to bring statues to life in the first century AD. Kroll remarks that it was common during this era for statues to be deemed able to speak and perform miracles. The Roman historian Dio Cassius records in detail how a foreign king, Tiridates, literally and publicly worshipped Nero and his images in one particular conference. A number of ancient and modern historians insist that those who refused to do so, both during and after Nero's reign, were executed.

David Chilton (quoting from English theologian Austin Farrer's 1964 work) points out that these executions were carried out not only by Roman authorities, but also by Jewish authorities aligned with Rome; "[The Jewish leaders] organized economic boycotts against those who refused to submit to [Nero] Caesar as Lord, the leaders of the synagogues 'forbidding all dealings with the excommunicated,' and going as far as to put them to death."

Revelation 13:16-17. And he causeth all, both small and great, rich and poor, free and bond, to receive a mark in their right hand, or in their foreheads: And that no man might buy or sell, save he that had the ***mark***, or the name of the beast, or the number of his name.

C. Marvin Pate and Calvin B. Haines Jr. (1995) record that those who worshipped Nero "received a certificate or mark of approval–

charagma, the same word used in *Revelation 13:16.*" Richard Anthony (2009) adds these details: "All those under the jurisdiction of Rome were required by law to publicly proclaim their allegiance to Caesar by burning a pinch of incense and declaring, 'Caesar is Lord'. Upon compliance with this law, the people were given a papyrus document called a 'libellus', which they were required to present when either stopped by the Roman police or attempting to engage in commerce in the Roman marketplace, increasing the difficulty of 'buying or selling' without this mark.

The following has been adapted from a lengthy article written by fellow Christian and researcher, Sam Rojahn.

> John's first-century readers, if they had wisdom and understanding, were to be able to identify the beast by calculating his number, which was "666." John wrote this as if the beast was already in power as he was putting these things down in writing. (Rev. 13:18).

> In Hebrew gematria, which John's readers would have been familiar with (given the vast number of Hebrew references in Revelation), Nero's name (NRWN QSR) = 666. The values of these seven Hebrew letters are 50, 200, 6, 50, 100, 60, and 200, respectively, adding up to 666. John's code would have utilized the Hebrew language rather than Greek or Latin in order to avoid detection from Roman authorities, being that he had been exiled to Patmos (a Roman prison island) by Rome.

> Nero's name also adds up to "616," which some early manuscripts refer to as the number of the beast because of a later transliteration into Latin. In this case "Nero Caesar" = 616 in Latin just as "Neron Caesar" = 666 in Hebrew, so Nero's identity is confirmed by both renderings.

> The beast was to have ten horns, which would carry it, give to it their own power and authority, persecute the saints, and finally turn on the "great prostitute" to the point of burning her with fire *(Rev. 13:1; 17:3, 7, 12-14, 16-17).*

> The Roman Empire contained 10 Senatorial Provinces, and the governors of each one granted their authority to Rome and also exercised authority on its behalf, This included aiding in Nero's persecution of the saints, and carrying out the Roman war against Israel which resulted in the burning of Jerusalem in 70 AD.

> The beast had seven heads. To John it was explained that the seven heads represented not only the "seven mountains on which the woman is seated," but also "seven kings, five of whom have fallen, one is [in John's day], the other has not yet come, and when he does come he must remain only a little while" (Rev. 13:1; 17:3, 7, 9-10).

Rome is the one city in history famous for its seven mountains, and first-century Rome celebrated the feast of the "seven-hilled city." According to Josephus, Dio Cassius, Suetonius, and other historians, the first five Roman emperors (or "kings"; cf. John 19:15) were [1] Julius Caesar [2] Augustus [3] Tiberius [4] Caligula, and [5] Claudius. The sixth was Nero (54-68 AD), and the next emperor was Galba, who reigned for only six months before he was murdered. The beast was to have a mouth like a lion (Rev. 13:2).

The apostle Paul, referring to his trial before Nero, testified that he was "rescued from the lion's mouth" *(2 Timothy 4:16-17)*.

One of the beast's heads was to receive a mortal wound, but the beast's wound would be healed, causing the whole earth to marvel "as they followed the beast" *(Rev. 13:3, 12)*.

Nero committed suicide in June 68 AD, bringing an end to the blood line that had sustained Rome since it had become an empire. His death was followed by chaos and civil war, causing the empire to nearly collapse, and Josephus testified that "every part of the habitable earth" under the Romans "was in an unsettled and tottering condition" (Wars 7.4.2).

The next three emperors (Galba, Otho, and Vitellius) each reigned considerably less than a year, each tried desperately to resurrect Nero's image and authority, and it was only when Vespasian came to power in December 69 AD that Rome stabilized and became more powerful than ever.

The "whole earth" would worship the beast, extolling it as incomparable and overwhelmingly powerful to any who would dare to oppose it. Only those whose names were "written before the foundation of the world in the book of life of the Lamb that was slain" would not worship the beast *(Rev. 13:4, 8; 17:8)*.

Nero demanded bizarre worship during his reign and this included offering sacrifices to Nero's spirit in the public square even after his death. One statue of Nero stood more than 110 feet high, and coins and other inscriptions hailed him as "Almighty God" and "Saviour." He was hailed as Apollo, Hercules, "the only one from the beginning of time," and even rulers from other lands had to publicly worship both Nero and his images which were set up on lofty platforms. As for the reference to "the whole earth," this can either be understood as referring to the Roman Empire *(cf. Luke 2:1)*, or to Israel.

In fact, multiple sources can be found on the Internet which would support the claim that Nero fulfilled the role of the man of sin. If not the literal character, then a spiritual being impersonating him, as a fake resurrected or reincarnated Nero. The image of the beast maybe? The first mention of the word "image" in the New Testament is used by Jesus when referring to the image and superscription on a coin. *(Matthew 22;20.)*

In September 2016, archaeologists discovered a gold coin in Jerusalem bearing the face of Nero, the Roman Emperor. The coin was likely struck in 56-57 AD, researchers say. This being around the time the Book of Revelation was most likely written.

Temple of God

I was also led to believe that a hypothetical third temple must be built in Jerusalem prior to the fulfilment of certain end time prophecy. A view shared by millions of Christians as I understand. For a third temple built in Jerusalem has become a central tenet for 'Zionism'.

Many Zionist Jews and Zionist Christians even compared Donald Trump to the Persian emperor, Cyrus the Great, who allowed the Jews to return from exile in Babylon to Israel, and build the second temple which was later destroyed in 70 A.D. As if expecting Trump to somehow pave the way for a new temple to be erected on the Temple Mount.

The Zionist rabbis have been talking about its construction for many decades now, but for the work to even begin, then surely the Islamic Al-Aqsa Mosque, which stands on the Temple Mount, must first be destroyed and millions of angry Muslims will have to die?

Certainly the Luciferian, 33 Degree Freemason and US Confederate war general, Albert Pike, predicted how a third world war will predominantly be fought between the Islamic leaders and the West.

Being realistic however, if we expect a literal third temple to be constructed in Jerusalem, prior to the fulfilment of virtually all other end-times prophecy leading up to the return of Christ and the rapture of believers, then we are seriously fast running out of time.

According to the apostle Paul, the return of Christ and the rapture can not occur until after the man of sin is revealed. Of this wicked man, Paul writes:

2 Thessalonians 2:4. Who opposeth and exalteth himself above all that is called God, or that is worshipped; so that he as God sitteth in the temple of God, shewing himself that he is God.

Many Christians believe Ezekiel's prophesied temple is symbolic, and RIGHTLY say, each individual Christian is the temple of God.

1 Corinthians 3:16. Know ye not that ye are the temple of God, and that the Spirit of God dwelleth in you?

I'm not sure about you, but personally I believe it would be an absolute travesty to equate the temple of God within which sits the deluded man of sin, with the physical body of one born of the Spirit.

The Protestant Reformers also rejected the idea of a literal temple being built in Jerusalem. They tended to believe that the Antichrist power would be revealed continually over the years, so that everyone would comprehend and recognize that the Pope is the real, true Antichrist and *not* the Vicar of Christ as the papacy claims.

Hence they believed that 'the man of sin', would be revealed to every generation down through the ages, in a continual succession of popes, culminating with the final pope aka *the* ultimate Antichrist.

Wrote Puritan minister Roger Williams in *The Prophetic Faith of Our Fathers*, Vol. 3, p. 52.

> The pretended Vicar of Christ on earth, who sits as God *over the Temple of God*, exalting himself not only above all that is called God, but over the souls and consciences of all his vassals, yea over the Spirit of Christ, over the Holy Spirit, yea, and God himself, speaking against the God of heaven, thinking to change times and laws; but he is the Son of Perdition.

The point being, no individual, no church or denomination, has a 100% monopoly on the interpretation of Scripture. The best one can offer is to compare scripture with scripture and use our God-given ability to reason from His word. Beyond human reasoning however, one can only trust that the Author himself, the Spirit of Truth, will guide us into all truth. *(John 16:13.)*

So how should we determine which temple of God Paul is referring to? A literal temple? Or a metaphorical temple? The King James Bible has a very organised vocabulary and never expects us to go outside of it to determine meaning. Thus the AKJV becomes its own interpreter.

The 'Law of First Mention' dictates a principle that requires one to go to that portion of the Scriptures where a subject first occurs, in order to establish the fundamental meaning of a particular thing.

Once that meaning has been firmly established, then continue with the same thought in mind wherever the subject is mentioned, unless the surrounding context dictates otherwise.

I believe this unwritten law is actually God's way of providing a correct understanding concerning the temple of God. For the term 'Temple of God' is not found anywhere in the Old Testament.

The first usage, or first mention in the Bible, is when Jesus enraged the Jewish Bankers and Traders of the day, by overturning their tables, in the literal physical temple.

Matthew 21:12 . And Jesus went into the temple of God, and cast out all them that sold and bought in the temple, and overthrew the tables of the moneychangers, and the seats of them that sold doves.

The term 'temple of God' appears nine times in the entire Bible, each in the New Testament. Five times it clearly refers to the body of Christ, or that of a born again believer, and twice to the temple of God in heaven.

Apart from first mention *(Matthew 21:12)* there is only one other verse where the term 'temple of God' is NOT used within a surrounding spiritual context. Hence we must apply the law of first mention and use the established meaning of a literal and physical temple.

2 Thessalonians 2:4. Who opposeth and exalteth himself above all that is called God, or that is worshipped; so that he as God sitteth in the temple of God,shewing himself that he is God.

Having used the Law of First Mention to establish how this act of blasphemy takes place in the *literal* temple of God, where does this prophecy fit in the timeline? Is this a still future event which takes place after a third temple has been built in Jerusalem?

No, this can't be the case, because this prophecy fulfilled back in the days of the second temple, which was destroyed with the fall of Jerusalem in 70 AD?

The Fall of Babylon

Because the Apostles and the early followers of Jesus believed that Jerusalem's days were numbered, is the most likely explanation for why beyond the four Gospels and the Book of Acts, physical Jerusalem barely gains a mention. From the Book of Romans onwards, physical Jerusalem is named on 9 occasions only, nine being the Biblical number associated with judgement, especially divine judgement.

In fact, when writing to the local church of which he was an elder, Peter refers to the city as Babylon. *(1 Peter 5:13.)*

Furthermore, the name 'Jerusalem' doesn't appear on a single occasion in the entire Book of Revelation. Instead John refers to her as, "the great city which spiritually is called Sodom and Egypt, where also our Lord was crucified" *(Revelation 11:8).*

It is not by chance, but by God's design that whilst never mentioned by name in the book of Revelations, Jerusalem is referred to as "that great city" on 6 occasions, and as "Babylon" 6 times in the 66th book of the Bible.

Be not deceived however, for over the course of history, the Biblical correlation between Jerusalem and end-times Babylon, has been deliberately suppressed. In fact, from the controllers point of view, it had to be suppressed. For if folk realised that Babylon had fallen over 2,000 years ago in 70 AD, they would also realize, or at least suspect, that the thousand year reign of the Lord Jesus Christ, may have already taken place.

A Thousand Years

The main purpose of Jesus' 1,000-year reign is to fulfil all the Old Testament prophecies given to Israel and the promises made to Jesus, the nations, and indeed, the whole earth.

In the history of Christian theology, three major millennial views have been advocated;namely premillennialism, postmillennialism and amillennialism. Simply put, Premillennialism is the belief that Jesus will physically return to the Earth *before* the Millennium, and usher in a literal thousand-year golden age of peace.

Postmillennialism sees Christ's second coming as occurring *after* the "Millennium", a Golden Age in which Christian ethics prosper. Amillennialism basically teaches that there will be no literal thousand year reign of the righteous on Earth.

Whatever view one holds however, it must be affirmed that Jesus Christ is ruling and reigning over all things *now*. For he has been exalted to God's right hand and must reign until *all* enemies are put under his feet, the last enemy being death. *(1 Cor. 15:25).* Death itself will not be destroyed until after the final judgement. *(Revelation 20:14.)*

Because it can be difficult to know when to take the Book of Revelation figuratively and when to take it literally, and because Revelation 20:1–6, is the only passage in Scripture that deals with the millennial reign of Christ explicitly, it becomes difficult to directly confirm one's point of view.

Nevertheless, because the term 'a thousand years' appears six times in Revelation 20, I feel there is no compelling reason to interpret the term in any other way than it being a literal thousand years.

For if God wished to communicate "a long period of time," he could easily have done so without explicitly and repeatedly mentioning an exact time-frame.

Preterism

I'm no expert on end-times prophecy by any stretch of the imagination, and lack the ability to offer an exposition on the Book of Revelations, or even prophecy in general. But maybe those who hold with the Preterist view (which I've always previously rejected) have been right about much all along.

Simply put, as an eschatological view, Preterism interprets some or even all prophecies of the Bible as events which have already happened. Nevertheless, **all** Scripture is profitable *(2 Timothy. 3:16)* even those parts of Scripture containing already fulfilled prophecies.

Historically, both preterists and non-preterists have generally agreed that the Jesuit, Luis de Alcasar (1554–1613) wrote the first systematic preterist exposition of prophecy which was published during the Counter-Reformation in the 16th century.

Should we dismiss his views immediately because the guy was a Jesuit? Or should we at least give him the benefit of the doubt, and consider why he made such a claim in the first place?

In the most general sense, Preterism refers to the view that a given future-oriented biblical text refers to an event that now lies in the *past*. Unlike 'Full Preteism' which sees ALL prophecy fulfilled, 'Partial' or 'Mild' Preterism only sees SOME prophecies fulfilled.

Whilst preterists disagree significantly about the exact meaning of the terms used to denote these divisions of preterist thought, all preterists agree that some of those that Jesus spoke to during his Olivet discourse, would still be alive to witness his coming in the clouds, as foretold by the prophet, Daniel.

In his book 'The Parousia' (p.361) J. Stuart Russell, a nineteenth-century preterist author, portrayed the Book of Revelation as being concerned "primarily and principally with events with which its first readers only were immediately interested, that is, the events all shortly to come to pass."

Indeed, John himself wrote how some prophetic events would occur *shortly* after he had recorded them, whilst others would transpire further down the line.

Revelation 1:1. The Revelation of Jesus Christ, which God gave unto him, to shew unto his servants things *which must shortly come to pass*; and he sent and signified [it] by his angel unto his servant John:

Revelation 1:19. Write the things which thou *hast seen*, and the things *which are*, and the things which shall be *hereafter*;

Hence, although it's generally taught the Book of Revelation was written somewhere around 95 A.D. most Preterists believe that because it speaks to particular circumstances and events that were fulfilled within the lifetime of the book's original first-century audience, its date of writing was most likely between 63 and 68 A.D. Other arguments for a preterist view of prophecy related to the Book of Revelation is because it was addressed to first century readers. Their proof lies in the seven churches which Jesus sends a message to. It's true, the book of Revelation does have a direct relevance to the original historical first century churches to whom it was addressed, and indeed, the text of the book itself points to the imminent fulfilment of many of its prophecies.

Yet it's also true that John's letters to the 7 churches in Asia are in a sense timeless, and in many ways relevant for every assembly of believers through the ages to this very day.

Of Full Preterism and concerning the Book of Revelation, former US pastor and theologian, John Walvoord wrote;

> The preterist view, in general, tends to destroy any future significance of the book, which becomes a literary curiosity with little prophetic meaning.

Yet of the mild version, American theologian, R.C. Sproul writes in his *The Last Days According to Jesus: (page158).*

> While partial preterists acknowledge that in the destruction of Jerusalem in A.D. 70 there was a parousia or coming of Christ, they maintain that it was not *the* parousia. That is, the coming of Christ in A.D. 70 was a coming in judgment on the Jewish nation, indicating the end of the Jewish age and the fulfillment of *a* day of the Lord. Jesus really did come in judgment at this time, fulfilling his prophecy in the Olivet Discourse. But this was not the final or ultimate coming of Christ. The parousia, in its fullness, will extend far beyond the Jewish nation and will be

universal in its scope and significance.

If I understand him correctly, Mr. Sproul is suggesting that the 70 AD judgement of the Jewish nation fulfilled *A* particular day of the Lord, as opposed to a future worldwide judgement on ***the*** day of the Lord, referred to as 'the great and the terrible day'. *(Joel 2:31)*.

Indeed, there are ***two*** specific days recorded in Scripture, each corresponding with a different event, and each seperate in time.

One is referred to as the 'day of Christ,' *(2 Thessalonians 2:2, Philippians 1:10 & 2:16)*. It's also known as the 'day of Jesus Christ' *(Philippians 1:6)*, the 'day of our Lord Jesus Christ' *(1Corinthians 1:8)*, or the 'day of the Lord Jesus' *(2Corinthians 1:14)*.

Without exception, the context surrounding each of these terms is one of hope, deliverance and blessing, such as;

Philippians 1:6. Being confident of this very thing, that he which hath begun a good work in you will perform it until the day of Jesus Christ:

Furthermore, the scriptures indicate that this remarkable day is a prelude to the redeemed appearing before the judgement seat of Christ. Here, rewards are received, or in some cases, maybe a loss of rewards, and should not be confused with the final judgement of souls at the great white throne. *(Revelation 20:11.)*

2 Corinthians 5:10. For we must all appear before the judgment seat of Christ; that every one may receive the things *done* in *his* body, according to that he hath done, whether *it be* good or bad.

1 Peter 5:4. And when the chief Shepherd shall appear, ye shall receive a crown of glory that fadeth not away.

The day of the Lord Jesus Christ, should not be mistaken for 'the day of the LORD' aka the day of the Lord, or 'the day of God', a day which is always associated with times of severe wrath and divine judgement, and which is described as 'great and terrible'.

2 Peter 3:10. But the day of the Lord will come as a thief in the night; in the which the heavens shall pass away with a great noise, and the elements shall melt with fervent heat, the earth also and the works that are therein shall be burned up.

Simply by way of reasoning from this one verse alone, the day of the Lord aka the day of God, cannot possibly be one and the same as the day of Christ. For if the heavens and the earth are burnt out of existence at his coming, how then can Jesus reign upon the earth for a thousand years?

The day of the Lord aka the day of God, occurs at some point in time **beyond** the one thousand years and **after** the little season when Satan is set free to deceive the nations once more.

Is it possible that we have all been hoodwinked in a way that beggars belief? That the end-time events which the majority of Christians believe are on the horizon, were actually fulfilled 2,000 years ago?

Hypothetically speaking, it could be argued that the simplest way to conceal the past fulfilment of any prophetic event, would be to manipulate the timeline. What better way of doing so, than to date the writing of that prophecy, as being two or three decades **after** the prophecy had actually come to pass? Would we be any the wiser today?

When Were the Gospels written?

"Got Questions" state;

> It is important to understand that the dating of the Gospels and other New Testament books is at best an educated guess and at worst foolish speculation. For example, suggested dates for the writing of the Gospel of Matthew range from as early as A.D. 40 to as late as A.D. 140.

> In the past many liberal theologians have argued for a later dating of many of the New Testament books than is probably warranted or valid, in an attempt to discredit or cast doubts upon the content and authenticity of the Gospel accounts.

> On the other hand, there are many scholars who look to a much earlier dating of the New Testament books. There are some that believe there is good evidence to support the view that the whole New Testament, including Revelation, was written prior to the destruction of Jerusalem in 70 A.D.

> It is our contention that the evidence supports the earlier dating more than it does the later dating.

In three of the gospels (Matthew, Mark and Luke) Jesus foretells of the coming destruction of the city of Jerusalem and its Temple, of times of severe hardship and persecution for his followers, and the rise of many false christs and false prophets etc.

Yet not once in the entire New Testament is the actual destruction of Jerusalem, recorded. This fact alone is a strong indicator that the entire New Testament was written and completed well before 70 AD.

Jesus refers to Jerusalem as "that great city" spiritually called Sodom and Egypt *(Revelation 11:8)* and Peter refers to Jerusalem as "Babylon".*(1 Peter 5:13.)*

In Revelation 1:1, we read how John was shown things WHICH MUST SHORTLY COME TO PASS.

Among other things, John foretells of the destruction of "that great city", Babylon.

Jerusalem is and always has been spiritual Babylon, and Jerusalem aka Babylon fell in 70 AD, and **after** the completion of the New Testament, which prophesied these events.

Don't be so ridiculous, you say?

Then ponder upon the words of Jesus, when warning his disciples of what **this generation**, might have to endure, and also be witness to.

Matthew 10:23. But when they persecute you in this city, flee ye into another: for verily I say unto you, *Ye shall not have gone over the cities of Israel*, till the Son of man be come.

*Matthew 13:41.*The Son of man shall send forth his angels, and they shall gather out of his kingdom all things that offend, and them which do iniquity;

Matthew 16:27. For the Son of man shall come in the glory of his Father with his angels; and then he shall reward every man according to his works.

Matthew 16:28. Verily I say unto you, There be *some standing here*, which shall not taste of death, till they see the Son of man coming in his kingdom.

Matthew 26:64. Jesus saith unto him, Thou hast said: nevertheless I say unto you, Hereafter shall ye see the Son of man sitting on the right hand of power, and coming in the clouds of heaven.

Matthew 23:36. Verily I say unto you, All these things shall come upon **this generation**.

Matthew 24:34. Verily I say unto you, *This generation* shall not pass, till *all these things* be fulfilled.

Luke 21:22. For these be the days of vengeance, that *all things which are written may be fulfilled.*

Mark 13:20. And except that the Lord had shortened those days, no flesh should be saved: but for the elect's sake, whom he hath chosen, he hath shortened the days.

Mark 13:26. And then shall they see the Son of man coming in the clouds with great power and glory.

Mark 13:27. And then shall he send his angels, and shall gather together his elect from the four winds, from the uttermost part of the earth to the uttermost part of heaven.

In Luke's account, and having just made the astounding statement, "and then shall they see the Son of man coming in a cloud with power and great glory", Jesus continues with; "And when these things begin to come to pass, then look up, and lift up your heads; for your *redemption* draweth nigh." *(Luke 21:28.)*

So likewise ye, when ye see these things come to pass, know ye that the kingdom of God *is nigh at hand.* Verily I say unto you, *This generation* shall not pass away, till all *be fulfilled. (Luke 21:31-32.)*

Who then, does "*this generation*" refer to? Those present with Jesus on the mount of Olives? Those who asked him if there would be signs to look out for, when Jesus foretold the destruction of the temple? Or those born in the future, long after the destruction of Jerusalem? I think Luke has already answered this question in previous chapters.

Luke 11:30. For as Jonas was a sign unto the Ninevites, so shall also the Son of man be to *this generation.*

Luke 11:50. That the blood of all the prophets, which was shed from the foundation of the world, may be required of *this generation;*

Luke 17:25. But first must he suffer many things, and be rejected of *this generation.*

Luke 21:22. For these be the days of vengeance, that *all things* which are written may be *fulfilled.*

By using the Biblical principle of establishing a matter from the mouth of two or three witnesses, Matthew, Mark and Luke are all in agreement; that some folk from *this generation* would still be alive to witness the coming of the Son of man in the clouds.

Because of statements like these, it would be foolhardy to even attempt to deny that the disciples all believed that Jesus would return whilst many of them would still be alive.

Son of Man

After his betrayal with a kiss in the garden of Gethsemane, Jesus was arrested and taken to stand before Caiaphas the high priest, where the scribes and the elders were assembled. Here Caiaphas confronted Jesus, and asked him straight out; 'Art thou the Christ, the Son of the Blessed?' *(Mark 14:61.)* To which Jesus replied; 'I am: and ye shall see the Son of man sitting on the right hand of power, and coming in the clouds of heaven'. *(Mark 14:62.)*

The fact that Caiaphas didn't believe him, is irrelevant. For Jesus was telling the Truth. But how about you and I? Do we believe Him? For if so, then Caiaphas was just one of the many thousands, who witnessed the fulfilment of Revelation 1:7.

'Behold, he cometh with clouds; and every eye shall see him, and they also which pierced him: and all kindreds of the earth shall wail because of him. Even so, Amen'.

When Jesus told those in his presence that some of them would still be alive to witness the Son of man coming in the clouds, and that all things that are written would be fulfilled, He was referring to the prophecy written by Daniel, a little under 500 years earlier.

Daniel 7:13. I saw in the night visions, and, behold, *one* like the Son of man came with the clouds of heaven, and came to the Ancient of days, and they brought him near before him.

All schools of eschatological thought agree, that the seventy weeks of Daniel 9:24, are to be prophetically understood as being a day for a year. Hence the seventy years of weeks; or 70x7 equals 490 years.

In 538 BC, the same year the Babylonian Captivity of the Jewish people formally ended, Daniel was given a prophecy by the angel, Gabriel. The prophecy of the 70 weeks summarizes what happens before Jesus sets up his millennial kingdom.

These seventy weeks of years (490 years) have already run their course, and have been fulfilled without error, in 27 AD, when Jesus Christ began his public ministry. *(Daniel 9:1-27.)*

Are we then to believe, that whilst Jesus claimed that *all things* which are written would be fulfilled, Daniel's prophecy was only fulfilled in part? Are we to believe that Jesus was *not* seen arriving in the clouds, as he had promised?

For this same Jesus, in his resurrected and glorified body, told John to record "things which shall be hereafter", which include his coming in the clouds.

Revelation 1:7. Behold, he cometh with clouds; and every eye shall see him, and they [also] which pierced him: and all kindreds of the earth shall wail because of him. Even so, Amen.

Even Old Testament prophecy fortold that the very same people who nailed their own Messiah to the Tree, would see him again thereafter, and wail and mourn over what they had done. *(Zechariah 12:10.)*

So yes, in view of the previously quoted scriptures, where Jesus clearly taught that some of those in his presence would still be alive and witness his coming in the clouds (as the Son of man), the ***past*** fulfilment view of prophecy is not only very hard to dismiss, it would also be quite illogical to do so. In fact, although it may sound rather harsh, one would have to be in a state of denial.

If by addressing "this generation" when he actually meant a distant future generation, it could even be said, that Jesus was guilty of misleading those present at the time. An impossibility, as I'm sure all would agree.

But remember, it's all too easy to only believe the parts of scripture that align with those things which we've previously been taught. It's called "inherited theology."

Christian preterists believe that the tribulation was a divine judgment visited upon the Jews for their sins, including their rejection of Jesus as the promised Messiah. It occurred entirely in the past, around 70 A.D. when the armed forces of the Roman Empire destroyed Jerusalem and its temple.

Which Jesus had foretold of course, nearly forty years earlier.

Again, because Jesus connected this coming judgment upon Jerusalem with his accession to the throne of the kingdom of God, a literal interpretation of the text would unarguably support the preterist view.

At Matthew 10:23, when Jesus said to his disciples; *"Ye shall not have gone over the cities of Israel, till the Son of man be come",* it is as good as certain to be a reference to Jesus's coming in judgment against Jerusalem in A.D. 70.

In fact it becomes very difficult to argue that Jesus was actually referring to folk who wouldn't be born for yet another two thousand years to come. So yes, if taken literally, a plain reading of Scripture would indeed indicate these prophecies have already been fulfilled. And yes, I'm fully aware that the past fulfilment of prophecy is a bitter pill to swallow, and likely many will reject it.

After his resurrection, the last words spoken by Jesus to his disciples, are recorded in the Book of Acts. When he had finished speaking, they witnessed Jesus ascending up to heaven in a cloud. As they were gazing upwards in amazement, two angels dressed in white clothing appeared, and said;

Ye men of Galilee, why stand ye gazing up into heaven? this same Jesus, which is taken up from you into heaven, shall so come in like manner as ye have seen him go into heaven. *(Acts 1:11.)*

Clearly they must have understood from these words, that just as they had seen Jesus ascend in a cloud, in time they would see him return in like manner.

I think it goes without saying, that these men to whom the angels appeared, would not have been able to stop talking about their recent experience. In all likelihood, the incredible news that Jesus would be returning in the clouds, spread like a raging wildfire across the entire community. Even to other nations, I dare say.

Certainly the generation Jesus spoke to at the time thought he was coming soon, and they got quite anxious whilst waiting. Which is why Peter records how a day to God is as a thousand years, so they wouldn't give up hope. *(2 Peter 3:8).*

And why Paul reminds those who were worried that they might have missed the day of Christ, how *that* day will *not* come until *after* the revealing of the man of sin and *after* a great falling away. *(2 Thessalonians 2:3).*

It would certainly seem that the apostle Paul was very optimistic when saying "*we* wich *are* alive" at the coming of Jesus. But he also offered words of comfort, and went on to explain that either way, alive or deceased, makes no difference. For the resurrection of all those who had previously died in faith, is coincident with the translation (or rapture) of the living.

1 Thessalonians 4:15 -17. For this we say unto you by the word of the Lord, that *we which are alive* and remain unto the coming of the Lord shall not prevent *them which are asleep.*

For the Lord himself shall descend from heaven with a shout, with the voice of the archangel, and with the trump of God: and *the dead* in Christ shall rise first:

Then *we which are alive* and remain shall be caught up *together* with *them* in the *clouds*, to meet the Lord in the air: and so shall *we* ever be with the Lord.

Whether this remarkable event occurred prior to, or at some point during the great tribulation, we are not told. However, the very words of the Lord Jesus, himself, should be enough to assure us, that Paul's prophecy was fulfilled during the lifetime of at least one of His original twelve disciples.

A brief recap of John chapter 21

I'm sure many are familiar with the third occasion when Jesus revealed himself to his disciples, after he had risen from the dead. But have we overlooked something of great relevance for us all today?

Thinking they would never see Jesus again, several of his disciples were aboard a ship, and had spent the night fishing, but thus far had caught nothing.

In the early morning they saw a man standing by the shore, but did not realize that this man was Jesus.*(21:3-4.)*

Having already told him they had no food to eat, Jesus then instructed the disciples to cast their nets to the right hand hand side, and before long, the nets were brimming with fish.

John was the first to realize that this man, whom they'd failed to recognize, was none other than the Lord Jesus, and told Peter so, who immediately jumped into the sea, and swam to the shore. *(21:5-7.)*

By the time the other disciples had also arrived to the shore, Jesus, in his new resurrected body, had already lighted a fire and was in the process of cooking a meal.

John 21:12. Jesus saith unto them, Come [and] dine. And none of the disciples durst ask him, Who art thou? knowing that it was the Lord.

Now let's jump forward a while, for having asked Peter three times, "do you love me?", Jesus foretold how Peter would die, but in the meanwhile, he must follow Jesus. *(John 21:18-19).*

Peter then asked Jesus about John, and what he was going to do. To which Jesus effectively said;

"If it is my will that John should tarry, or wait till I come, never you mind, for I want you to follow me".

Could it be, that just like the early disciples, we too, have not grasped a full understanding, of what Jesus was actually saying?

John 21:23. Then went this saying abroad among the brethren, that that disciple should not die: yet Jesus said **not** unto him, He shall not die; **but**, If I will that he **tarry till I come**, what [is that] to thee?

For here's the thing; Peter would follow Jesus, and eventually suffer and die, and in such a manner which would bring glory to God. *(John 21:19.)* Whilst John himself would not die, but would wait for the coming of Jesus. *(John 21:22.)*

Is John still alive on earth today? Obviously not, but unless Jesus made a big mistake, John had tarried, or waited until Jesus had come.

After his death, Peter would have been numbered amongst "the dead in Christ", while John would have been numbered with those "which are alive and remain." Yet both Peter and John, would have been caught up together in the clouds, to meet the Lord in the air. *(1 Thessalonians 4:16-17.)*

Mark 13:26. And then shall they see the Son of man coming in the clouds with great power and glory.

Mark 13:30. Verily I say unto you, that this generation shall not pass, till all these things be done.

A hard and bitter pill to swallow, I know. But most of the prophetic events that most of us have been taught are still future, were perfectly fulfilled prior to, or coincident with, the fall of that great city in 70 AD.

Revelation Chapter 14 is set on the **earth, prior** to the first resurrection, and during the great tribulation, as it is brought to an end. It describes the rebellion against God at Armageddon, the victory of Jesus Christ and the fall of Babylon (Jerusalem.)

Revelation Chapter 19 is set in **heaven, after** the first resurrection and the bodily translation of believers, known as the rapture. It describes the marriage supper of the Lamb, and how the armies of heaven (the resurrected saints) in their new glorified bodies, follow Jesus as he returns to earth in vengeance as the Word of God and with a name which is unknown to man.

John's portrayal of the end time judgments and the return of Christ as the Word of God are unmistakable, but for obvious reasons no specific dates or times are given, apart from the one thousand years.

In view of His promise, that some would still be alive to witness his coming, it is now my understanding that the first resurrection and rapture of believers occurred on the day of Christ, aka the day of the Lord Jesus, when he returned in the clouds as the Son of Man.

Revelation 19:14. And the armies *which were* in heaven followed him upon white horses, clothed in fine linen, white and clean.

This was most likely toward the end of the great tribulation, and coincident with the fall of Jerusalem aka Babylon in 70 A.D.

In other words, the events by far the majority of Christians are anticipating today, actually took place over 2,000 years in the past.

Events so huge they could not just be dismissed and swept under the carpet, but have been disguised in our history books as the Great Fire of Rome in 64 A.D, followed by the destruction of Jerusalem in 70 A.D. (which Jesus had foretold), and the decline of the Western Roman Empire,over the next few hundred years.

In reality, the approximate 6 year period between the destruction of these two major cities, may well have been the time of the Great Tribulation.

The most influential false Christ that Jesus had previously warned of, was undoubtedly Simon bar Kochba, whose followers revolted against Roman authority, which directly led to the death of 580,000 Jews. The resulting disease and famine in desolated Judea killed far more.

The Historical Record

Three different historians recorded that Jesus, followed by an army of angels, appeared over Jerusalem during Passover, three and a half years before its destruction in 70 AD. Furthermore, the parallels between these three historic accounts with Revelation 19 is quite remarkable.

Writes *Josephus in The Wars of the Jews (6.5.3);*

> On the twenty-first day of the month of Artemisius [Jyar], a certain prodigious and incredible phenomenon appeared; I suppose the account of it would seem to be a fable, were it not related by those that saw it, and were not the events that followed it of so considerable a nature as to deserve such signals; for, before sunsetting, chariots and troops of soldiers in their armor were seen running about among the clouds, and surrounding of cities

Tacitus records in *The Histories (5.13)*

"In the sky appeared a vision of armies in conflict, of glittering armour."

Pseudo-Hegesippus also describes the coming of Christ on the clouds with His mighty angels, when in *Pseudo-Hegesippus 44.* he writes,

> A certain figure appeared of tremendous size, which many saw, just as
> the books of the Jews have disclosed, and before the setting of the sun
> there were suddenly seen in the clouds chariots in the clouds and armed
> battle arrays by which the cities of all Iudaea and its territories were
> invaded.

The medieval Jewish historian Sepher Yosippon expounds upon this
angelic army in the sky of AD 66 by saying;

> Moreover, in those days were seen chariots of fire and horsemen, a
> great force flying across the sky near to the ground coming against
> Jerusalem and all the land of Judah, all of them horses of fire and riders
> of fire.

Yosippon's description of the angelic army of fire in the sky in 66
AD, fulfils the prophecies of the coming of the Lord in Isaiah 66:15,
Psalm 68:17 and Habakkuk 3:1-8 in a surprisingly literal way.

Diferring Views

Full or extreme preterism denies the physical reality of Christ's
second coming, claiming instead that the coming of Christ was one
of a spiritual, or invisible nature, as too is the thousand year reign.

It is possible of course, that Jesus did indeed reign invisibly for one
thousand years from the position of the Government in Heaven
above. Whilst the kings and priests of God reigned on the earth
below.

Yet this has to be balanced with the fact that prophecy about Jesus
Christ in the Old Testament was fulfilled literally. Jesus' birth,
ministry, death, and resurrection all occurred exactly as the Old
Testament predicted. The prophecies were literal.

Incidentally, Post Millennialists also say that we're already past the
1000 year reign of Christ. Or at least, that we're currently living in it.
Thus, as far as I can see, one's own personal eschatological
viewpoint is often based more upon inherited theology, rather than a
literal understanding of the word of God.

Jesus tells us that Truth sets us free. It's been quite a struggle along
the way, but do feel I'm now free from the futurist interpretation of
much of the end-time prophecies. For the generation that would
witness his coming as the Son of man in the clouds, were those in
his presence at the time. Not some remote generation of believers
2,000+ years in the future.

What length of time passes between Jesus coming as the Son of man and the start of the one thousand year reign, we are not told. It could have started immediately, or within a few days, weeks, months, or even several years.

One form of mild preterism claims that the fulfilment of certain eschatological passages occurred during the first three centuries, culminating with the fall of Rome in the Fourth Century AD.

If this understanding is correct, and if the millennial reign began around the same time, then from a past fulfilment view of prophecy, the literal one thousand years came to an end during the fourteenth Century.

Others believe the millennial kingdom began around 76 AD, hence would have extended until 1076 AD. Because it appears that a minimum of 700 years are effectively missing from history, by adding those 'missing' years back into the timeline, we arrive at 1776 AD.

This is all theoretical of course, I'm just throwing it out there as food for thought, so to speak. Some might even say;'Way too far out'.

In That Day

Zechariah 14;9. And the LORD shall be king over all the earth: in that day shall there be one LORD, and his name one.

Revelation 19:16. And he hath on [his] vesture and on his thigh a name written, KING OF KINGS, AND LORD OF LORDS.

Revelation 20:6. Blessed and holy *is* he that hath part in the first resurrection: on such the second death hath no power, but they shall be priests of God and of Christ, and shall reign with him a thousand years.

Revelation 5:10. And hast made us unto our God kings and priests: and *we shall reign on the earth.*

Each resurrected believer who has returned to earth, now has a new name, and even Jesus himself returned with a name unknown to mankind. *(Revelation 2:17.)*

Those resurrected and translated, have now received their new immortal and glorified bodies which make them like the angels. Who neither marry or are given in marriage. *(Matthew 22:30.)*

We are given no reason whatsoever to believe that those who rule the earth as kings and priests of God, will do so adorned with literal priestly robes and a regal crown. On the contrary, the Bible informs us that the believer's new resurrected body will be of an immortal and spiritual nature, just like the glorious resurrected body of Jesus. *(Philippians 3:21.)*

After his resurrection, Jesus was not restricted by the natural laws of physics. He still retained visible wounds and his disciples could physically touch him, yet he was able to travel effortlessly and appear and disappear at will. He could go through walls and doors, yet could also eat and drink and sit and talk.

These resurrected kings and priests may well appear as men amongst men, but nevertheless, men of God gifted with great power and authority, and with wisdom and knowledge, as a spiritual crown.

Effectively, a completely new classification of beings, often, but not always depicted with halos or auras of light around their heads, and generally referred to as saints. Men whose bodies had been changed by God from the corruptible to the incorruptible, from the mortal to the immortal in "the twinkling of an eye". *(1 Corinthians 15:52.)*

Although the years of great tribulation, which terminate with the battle of Armageddon, brings worldwide desolation of cataclysmic

179

proportions, according to the Scriptures, there would still be a few survivors.(*Isaiah 24:6.)*

Those who survived the great tribulation will continue in their mortal bodies, marrying and bearing children, but everyone on earth will enjoy the blessings of life as promised by God.

That's not to say those in ***mortal*** bodies would be perfect of course, for in their fallen state, mankind would still struggle with sin and eventually die. However they would live their lives unhindered by ***direct*** temptation from Satan, who remains bound for the entire one thousand years. *(Revelation 20:3.)*

Isaiah envisions a humanity marked by its prosperity and longevity *(Isaiah 65:22)*. In fact, those in mortal bodies will die prematurely at the relatively young age of 100 years. Much like a child dying without having fulfilled his days. *(Isaiah 65:20)*. The prophet also indicates that crop farming and house building will be a widespread industry. *(Isaiah 2:4. Is. 65:21.)*

At times it can be difficult to know whether or not to take a passage in the Bible literally. Although more often than not, the scriptures can have both a literal and a metaphorical, or spiritual meaning.

Zechariah 14:8, informs us that ***in that day***, and regardless of which of the seasons, rivers of ***living waters*** will go out from Jerusalem, both to the former and the hinder sea, which is generally understood to mean both eastward and westward. Metaphorically, the living waters refer to the Holy Ghost, which was first received by believers on the day of Pentecost. *(Acts 2:4.)* These living waters have since been freely available to anyone on earth who comes to faith in Jesus Christ.

Yet could this verse also have a literal or physical meaning? Were those who lived on earth during the millennial reign blessed with literal living waters? Could it be that many of the old legends are based upon a truth beyond our comprehension? The thirteenth century St. Francis of Assisi for example, who talked to the birds and befriended the wild animals?

Again, Isaiah 11:6-9 envisions a time when there will be harmony within the animal kingdom. They will all live together peacefully and without fear of man.

It's even quite likely that the legendary tale of St. George slaying the dragon, which dates back prior to 300 AD, alludes to Jesus casting

Satan, the dragon, into the abyss. *(Revelation 20:2.)*For St. George is usually depicted with an aura of light around his head, riding a white horse and wielding a long sword.

During the millennium, Jesus rules the nations with an iron rod *(Revelation 19:15)* and the resurrected believers whom he has made kings and priests unto God, shall reign upon the earth for a thousand years. *(Revelation 5:10).*

For a period of a thousand years there will be a rule of righteousness on earth, but during an age which is ***not*** under the Mosaic Law. For the law was perfectly fulfilled by Jesus during his lifetime. Jesus also fulfilled the sacrificial system of the Old Covenant by His death on the tree. *(Hebrews 1:3, 7:27, 9:12, 9:24-28).*

The whole world will prosper and be at peace, but the surviving inhabitants of the nations are required to make an annual pilgrimage to Jerusalem to worship the King, the Lord of hosts, and to celebrate the Feast of Tabernacles. *(Zechariah 14:16.)* As far as I'm aware, the Bible gives no indication that any other celebration or feast day is observed during the millennium.

The fact however, that people from every nation come to Jerusalem most likely does not mean that every individual on earth ***must*** travel to Jerusalem during the millennium, because physical Jerusalem had been destroyed

Most likely, people will be able to worship the Lord from anywhere in the world: "For the earth shall be filled with the knowledge of the glory of the LORD, as the waters cover the sea." *(Habakkuk 2:14.)*

Yet we are told that families and nations who refuse to do so, will suffer severe drought conditions and food shortages, for there will be no rainfall on their land during that year.*(Zechariah 14:16-17).*

Interestingly, in 2018, medieval scholar Michael McCormick nominated 536A.D. as "the worst year to be alive" because much of the world went dark for a full 18 months, as a mysterious fog rolled over Europe, the Middle East and parts of Asia.

Wrote Byzantine historian Procopius of Caesarea;*"The sun gave its light without brightness, like the moon, during this whole year."*

We are told the extreme weather event was ***probably*** caused by a huge volcanic eruption early in the year, causing average summer temperatures to fall 1.5°C to 2.5°C, resulting in drastic crop failures and severe famine for well over a year.

This could well be a smokescreen of course. For severe famine due to crop failure, could equally be caused by zero rainfall during the year. Which if the case, is hardly likely to be recorded in the official historical record.

Over the entire duration of the one thousand years, the old Serpent, Satan, will no longer be able to deceive the nations, for he will be imprisoned within the bottomless pit. *(Revelation 20:2).*

However, even with Satan bound, it's quite possible there were many skirmishes and conflicts along the way, the true nature of which, remains unclear. What was the true purpose behind the Crusades for example? All we really know for certain is that the city of Jerusalem played a pivotal role. Or has even this period of history been fabricated by the controllers, to provide a false narrative to disguise the annual pilgrimage to Jerusalem?

To my knowledge the Bible doesn't mention exactly where they go to, but nevertheless, at the end of the millennium the saints in their glorified bodies leave this earthly aeon, *world* or habitable age. Yet although we are left to presume they return to heaven, Revelation 20:9 indicates "the camp of the saints" is located somewhere on Earth.

Neither are we told the run of events leading up to the end of the thousand years. Is it a gradual ending? Or is it an abrupt one? Is Satan released from the bottomless pit immediately? Or are the restraints gradually removed? Nobody knows.

Power Vacuum

Many believe that at some point in time after the millennium a cataclysmic worldwide event took place, although there's a conflict of opinion over the cause. In the aftermath, warring political and religious factions fought to gain control of individual kingdoms and nation-states.

Why did Napoleon appear on the scene in the nineteenth century to allegedly destroy half of Europe? Or was this in part a fabricated version of history to cover up a cataclysmic event that had recently occurred in Europe?

This battle for power and control resulted in a Great Reset, under the guise of Roman Catholicism, Imperialism and Colonialism. From which point, a kind of worldwide land raid began, to grab the countries of the world that had been devastated by the catastrophe.

Writes gifted researcher of alternative history, Michelle Gibson at piercingtheveilofillusion.com;

> The year of 1493 was the year that Pope Alexander VI authorized the land-grab of the Americas in the "Inter Cetera"papal bull. This papal bull became a major document in the development of subsequent legal doctrines regarding claims of empire in the "New World" and assigned to Castile in Spain the exclusive right to acquire territory, to trade in, or even approach the lands laying west of the meridian situated one-hundred leagues west of the Azores and Cape Verde Islands, except for any lands actually possessed by any other Christian prince beyond this meridian prior to Christmas, 1492.

The Emperor of the Roman Empire became the Pope of the Roman Catholic Church. The famous Papal Bull 'Unam Sanctam', supposedly dating back to the Middle Ages, was intended to cement the absolute rule of the Pope. The last sentence of this bull reads;

> But we now declare, say and define that it is absolutely necessary for salvation for every human creature to be subject to the Roman Pontiff.

"Thus the Pope legitimized himself as the sole representative of God on earth by assuming the title, 'The Vicar of Christ'. At the same time, the so-called "heretical" Christian communities, such as the Albigensians and Cathars, condemned the papacy as the church of the Antichrist, and considered themselves the successors of the true Christian heritage, which, however, was only allowed to continue in secret."

"European colonialism intentionally created divides over almost the entire landmass of the earth, creating new countries from lands that were taken, as well as divisions and discords between peoples that originally existed in harmony worldwide. It also diagrams the means by which power and control were consolidated worldwide, mostly starting out as "trading" companies that ended up being very powerful in their respective regions, and after gaining complete control, transferring power and control of the regions to their respective European empires." *(Credit:Michelle Gibson.)*

In 1744, Mayer Amschel Rothschild was born in Frankfurt, and went on to become the founder of the Rothschild banking dynasty.

He also financed the Jesuit-trained Adam Weishaupt, who in 1776, and coincident with the founding of the United States of America, founded the infamous, quasi-masonic society called the Covenant of Perfectibility (Perfectibilists). This was later changed to the Order of Illuminati in 1778.

Between 1876 and 1915 a full one-quarter of the earth's surface lost their old governments and got conquered by the imperial forces. This power shift sealed the fate of all the independent kingdoms and empires on earth, as the old-world lifestyle focused on the quiet life of sustainable agriculture, arts, tradition and religion, while keeping politics and military at a minimum, no longer worked.

Strangely enough, over the same general time period, a new breed of rulers, or controllers emerged; extremely wealthy and powerful families, commonly referred to as the 'Black Nobility.' These families supported the Popes in the governance of the Papal States and in the administration of the Holy See.

The Hohenzollern and Orange-Nassau black nobility families simultaneously controlled Britain, the Netherlands, the German Empire, as well as the Russian Tsarist Empire. The Habsburgs, funded by the Fuggers, controlled Central Europe, the Vatican and parts of Western Europe. The Catholic-Protestant war zones created across Europe in the 1600's were transported to Ireland and right across to America.

Many of their descendants today, choose to remain anonymous and are rarely seen by the public, hence why most have never heard of them. They have an almost unbelievable amount of power and control over the affairs of this world.

The Chigi-Albani della Rovere family for example, who on behalf of Arturo Sosa (the Jesuit Black Pope) control the 'Equestrian Order of the Holy Sepulchre of Jerusalem'. Or the Sforza family who control worldwide media. Which is why virtually all mainstream news channels speak in unison, when reporting on matters such as the war in the Ukraine, Covid and Vaccines etc.

All have likely heard of Anthony Fauci however, who was one of the main controllers of the fraudulent Covid pandemic narrative. His mother's maiden name was Abys, daughter of Black Nobility, Giovanni and Raffaela Abys. The family crest of both the Abys and the Sforza family, depicts a Crowned Serpent devouring a young child.

For first and foremost, this is a Spiritual War of lies and deceit, where the souls of mankind are at stake. Have no doubt, the controllers of the official narrative work on behalf of the enemy of souls, "that old serpent, which is the Devil, and Satan". *(Revelation 20:2).*

Bound together by blasphemous secret society oaths, they are the ones responsible for instigating and financing both sides of every war upon earth since the French Revolution of 1789.

They give themselves Nobel peace prizes, honorary PhDs, Cabinet positions, UN leadership roles, University chairs, Supreme and World Court positions, and an assortment of humanitarian awards. They make the laws, interpret the laws, and let each other violate the laws at will. They claim to be indignant toward the suffering and poverty of people of other nations. Yet remain indifferent to the misery and poverty they inflict upon their own people.

They make weapons, run the military and sign peace accords. They start world wars, and then claim to want world peace.

They swear to God and seek the light of Lucifer.

A Little Season

Hypothetically then, if there has been a 1000 year period fitting such a description during the last 2,000 years or so, surely there'd be a record of it? Wouldn't there?

Quite frankly, I'm not so certain. Not a blatantly obvious record anyway. Remember, this is the same crafty old serpent who, starting in the garden of Eden, has deceived individuals and nations for millennia. He also has the ability to transform into an angel of light. *(2 Corinthians 11:14)*. Little wonder so many cults and religions began with a visiting angel over the last few centuries.

For you see, at the end of the thousand years with redeemed men in glorified bodies ruling the earth as kings and priests of Jesus Christ, Satan is loosed from his prison "for a little season". Why? For the very purpose of deceiving individuals and all the nations of the earth once again. One can only speculate the reason for this.

Many see the release of Satan as one last chance to show humanity that they have no real excuse for rejecting the truth of God. For if people only knew that God existed, then they would believe in Him.

However, the Bible says otherwise, that man has no excuse for unbelief, because all the evidence he needs for a Creator can be witnessed in the creation around him. *(Romans 1:20)*.

Personally, and assuming the one thousand year reign has already occurred, I suspect things had reached a point where a large percentage of the world's population began to resent being ruled with a rod of iron. And subservient to the kings and priests of Jesus Christ.

Much like the response from the general public in the parable of the nobleman who travelled to a far country to inherit a kingdom and return.

Luke 19:14. But his citizens **hated** him, and sent a message after him, saying, We will **not** have this *man* to reign over us.

We're told that having been released, Satan is only permitted a ***little season*** in which to carry out his deceptive plans. *(Revelation 20:3.)*

But not told the length of time the 'little season' refers to. A few months perhaps? Several years or decades maybe? Or could the little season amount to a number of centuries?

All we know is, that during this allotted period of time, Satan will deceive every individual and nation on earth which will culminate in the gathering all of the nations together (collectively called Gog and Magog) for the final battle on Earth against Jesus Christ.

It seems that God will not allow this final war to escalate, and deals with this rebellious confederation of nations promptly, by sending fire down from heaven to destroy them.

Revelation 20:7. And when the thousand years are expired, Satan shall be loosed out of his prison,

Revelation 20:8. And shall go out to deceive the nations which are in the four quarters of the earth, Gog and Magog, to gather them together to battle: the number of whom *is* as the sand of the sea.

Revelation 20:9. And they went up on the breadth of the earth, and compassed the camp of the saints about, and the beloved city: and fire came down from God out of heaven, and devoured them.

Nobody really knows what "the camp of the saints" and the "blessed city" actually refer to, or even where they are located. For neither term appears anywhere else in the Bible, to provide a cross reference. To assume the blessed city refers to Jerusalem when Jesus calls her "Spiritually Sodom and Egypt" *(Revelation 11:8.),* is probably unwise.

This final battle will be short-lived however, and is followed by Divine fiery destruction and the final resurrection of the dead, to judgement at the Great White Throne. *(Revelation 20:8-11.)*

At a guess, I suspect such a worldwide deception would likely run into centuries rather than a few years or decades.

Either way, I think it goes without saying, that Satan and his Luciferian priesthood, would go the extra mile to conceal the fact that the kings and priests of Jesus Christ had reigned upon the earth for a thousand years, whilst he himself had been chained up for the entire duration, within the bottomless pit.

What better way of doing so, than by manipulating the historical record, and destroying any evidence which suggest that events of the past were far different to what we've been led to believe.

Book burning was the most common form of censorship in the past. Apart from the official Vatican Library, it's believed by many, that possibly millions of ancient texts, manuscripts and other documents are hidden away in the underground catacombs of Vatican City.

Who knows whether or not every account and written record of the millennial reign has been removed from the public domain?

My point being, how can we know for certain whether or not we personally, and even the 5 or 6 generations before us have been born into the time period known as the little season? All we can know for certain is the day, the year and the century we and our immediate forbears were born in.

We would have no way of knowing whether or not there was a Great Reset of sorts a couple of centuries ago, if there is no official historical record for it. Or even if the historical record has been fabricated to such an extent, with the sole intention of keeping us in the dark concerning past events.

We're talking of a time remember, prior to the invention of the camera, and without mass media coverage. On the other hand, maybe there is evidence, albeit disguised, re-dated and redesignated to fit a more acceptable version of history.

Evidence that has always been right in front of our eyes, but we fail to see it, because by rights, the evidence should not be there.

For is it possible that these kings and priests of God, who in their glorified bodies were like the angels, were the true builders of the architectural wonders of the old world? Repurposed buildings we now call Palaces, Mansions and Cathedrals etc. Buidings of such finery and grandeur, which we are told were constructed in an impossible manner by peasants with a collection of primitive hand tools, during the age of the horse and cart?

Magnificent structures, built for a noble purpose, by those of the *first* resurrection in their *glorified* bodies, and since inherited by men with *mortal* bodies during "the little season", which began with the release of the old Serpent, the Dragon, the great Deceiver?

Is it possible that for a period of one thousand years, those who were born into this world and inhabited the earth in their mortal bodies, enjoyed a peaceful existence and the blessing of a world-wide free electro-magnetic energy grid?

A world in which water, sound and frequency played a major role? A world that by and large, has been deleted from the official record?

Inversion

Is it possible that the Tartarian kingdom, which so many are talking about right now, is merely the scapegoat for a world ruled for one thousand years by the kings and priests of Jesus Christ?

The further one ventures down the Rabbit Hole, the more things become turned upside down or inverted.

Could it be that a presumed Tartarian race of people, is receiving the credit for tens of thousands of magnificent buildings across the world, that would be as good as impossible for mortal men to build at the time?

This is how the occult magicians work; they masquerade as the exact opposite of what things truly are. For Tartaria comes from the same root as Tartarus, meaning the deepest region of Hell.

It's difficult to ascertain exactly where the medieval state of Tartaria was located, yet it seems to have reached its peak with the Mongolian Empire. Apparently Mongolian or Mongol refers to the State and Tartar or Tartarian to the Population.

The term "to catch a Tartar" means to catch hold of something that cannot be controlled, and is thought to have originated in the 1660's. Around the time of the Great Fire of London.

Over the course of the nineteenth and early twentieth century, the masterminds of enlightenment through science, such as Darwin and Einstein, have inverted the truth of creation, and the uniqueness of man created in the image and likeness of God. In their nihilistic world-view, man is a meaningless product of evolution, adrift on a random, spinning ball of rock, in an endless, cold and dark universe.

The so-called Big Bang theory is a good example to understand how religious-esoteric concepts entered science. In 1931, the Belgian, Jesuit priest Georges Lemaitre, created the Big Bang theory.

Not on the basis of scientific facts, but on the basis of a religious conviction, a notion of a primordial or cosmic seed from which everything evolved. Ironically, the theory is accepted by nearly all astronomers today, even though not a single proof has ever been presented.

Just like the staged moon landing, evolution, the globe earth, heliocentricity and the big bang, all are science fiction. Now in the 21st century, yesterday's science fiction has become today's reality, in the form of an injectable, so-called 'medical cure', in the form of self-assembling nano-technology, designed to connect humanity with the Internet Of Things.

Maybe we get what we deserve for believing all of their lies and propaganda. Instead of trusting and believing in Jesus Christ, the Word of God, who warns us that the god of this world and the Synagogue of Satan are liars. *(Revelation 3:9.)*

Food For Thought

According to the official narrative, the earliest recorded inhabitants of the British Isles were pagans, who worshipped many different gods and supernatural forces. It's generally understood, that stories of a man named Jesus, arrived at England's shores with the Romans in the first century A.D. but those stories were interspersed with multiple Roman deities. Although there's evidence for Christianity in England dating back to the late second century, it wasn't until the late sixth century, when the gospel of Jesus Christ first came to the Anglo-Saxons, and the conversion to Christianity began.

The Tyndale Bible (c. 1522–1536) is credited with being the first Bible translation in the English language to work directly from the Hebrew and Greek texts. This was followed by the Authorised King James Version of the Bible in 1611. Christianity was then introduced to North America as it was colonized by the Europeans beginning in the 16th and 17th centuries.

The point being, it's highly unlikely that the average person living in the first few centuries had even heard of Israel and Jerusalem, let alone were aware that the city had been ransacked by the Romans around 1,500 years earlier in 70 A.D.

Bear in mind the Crusades didn't start until 1095 A.D. a little over one thousand years since the destruction of Jerusalem. Or have the crusades been fabricated to bulk out the time-line corresponding with the end of the millennial reign?

Again the point being, that the earliest date for anyone in the western world, to have gained even the most basic understanding of Biblical end-times prophecy, would have been shortly before the Great Fire of London in 1666, the fire which burned from September 2 to September 5, and consumed five-sixths of the City.

Could this be yet another false narrative; a cover story to justify the destruction of much of the old world architecture and infrastructure in London? Was the Great Fire a controlled burn event, in which some of the old world structures were spared and repurposed?

The magnificent St. Paul's Cathedral for example, since credited to Christopher Wren. Many are convinced that not only was Wren a Freemason, he was also a Grand Master. Many have long believed that the great fire of London was an act of arson carried out by the Jesuits. The monument in the City of London about the London fire of 1666 still read until 1830;

"The most terrible destruction of this city; begun and carried on by the treachery and wickedness of the papal faction."

At the same time, is it possible the Great Fire of London was a cover story, and one used to disguise a major catastrophe of an entirely different nature?

The "Middle Ages" came to a tumultuous end, with deliberately planned famine, plague, revolts and war. It is estimated that the 'Black Death' alone, killed more than half of the European and North African population, and over one third of the middle east.

As the old medieval age began to fall slowly away into obscurity, it was gradually replaced with the period known as the Renaissance. Yet this supposed age of enlightenment, also produced a dark shadow, one that effectively rose again

A shadow entity that began implementing a long-term plan that is still in action today. This shadow entity has one end goal, world domination, a Great Reset, or New World Order if you like.

Its other primary objective, was to erase and fabricate much of the history of the age which had gone before, known as the medieval period A new style of architecture and pseudo-stone masonry was devised, namely the 'New Classical', a mixture of Romanesque, Gothic and Moorish style.

Most likely starting in Florence, Italy, the demolishing of the old sites, and replacing them with this new style of architecture, soon spread right across Europe, and then to the rest of the world.

If the intricate architecture of the grand cathedrals etc. had ever held an alternative and far grander function, such as energy-gathering, storage and distribution, it was lost here, during the Renaissance.

If indeed, Britain and America have a greater hidden history, it too, was lost or disguised here.

Unanswered Questions

Why was there such a massive, and virtually unexplained increase in the number of people afflicted by severe mental health and emotional issues in the mid-nineteenth century? By concentrating mainly on the UK and America, I've barely scratched the surface on this one.

For whatever event, or series of events may have taken place to cause this unexplained phenomena, it seems to have affected most, if not the entire world, at more or less the same time.

Asylums for those deemed to be Insane, opened their doors in France, Belgium, Germany, Spain, Portugal, Italy, Russia, Canada, Australia, New Zealand and most other nations, all around the same time period.

The number of folk treated in asylums increased exponentially from the middle of the nineteenth century, with the number rising in France from 10,000 patients in 1840 to over 60,000 in 1900.

Asylums grew ever larger and took on gigantic proportions, often surpassing 1,000 patients. One such example is the Asile Sainte-Anne Lunatic Asylum at Clermont, located in the Oise department in northern France, which for a long time was Europe's largest institution for the mentally ill. *(Credit:Wikipedia.)*

An ariel photograph taken from a hot air balloon in 1887 shows the sheer size of the complex, which set in 26 acres of rural countryside, consists of an entire array of old world buildings.

Judging by the scale and the number of buildings, it was most likely an old world power generating plant, and a massive farm combined. Now repurposed to house thousands of mentally ill patients.

Australia's first major asylum opened in 1867, in Ararat, Victoria. At its height, the Ararat Lunatic Asylum was massive, and consisted of 70 buildings which housed up to 1,000 patients.

In early colonial New Zealand, those deemed "lunatic" were initially housed in town gaols along with petty thieves, debtors, drunkards and vagrants. It wasn't until 1846, that the first of many asylums was established.

At this time in history, there were 125 legitimate reasons to be put into asylums. Those reasons included laziness, bad habits, jealousy, disappointment, time of life, imaginary female troubles, gatherings in the head, political excitement and religious enthusiasm, to name but a few.

In fact, there were enough categories, many of which were quite outrageous, to cover virtually any given circumstance. In other words, all governments now had a legitimate reason to send virtually anyone, from any walk of life, to a lunatic asylum.

Who defined the meaning of "gatherings in the head", "religious enthusiasm" or "political excitement" for example? For such terms could be applied to any individual who disagreed with, or objected to any decision or action carried out by their respective government.

The authorities evidently placed people in these institutions for just about any little thing. But they also experimented on many of these people, possibly to cause them to forget.

The history of electric shock therapy, or electric convulsion therapy (ECT) is highly disturbing. ECT was invented in Italy in 1938. In 1939 it was brought to England and replaced cardiazol (metrazol) as the preferred method of inducing seizures in convulsion therapy.

Both treatments (chemical and electrical) produced the same nasty side effects; namely seizures, often uncontrollable, followed by amnesia. The average age of patients receiving this treatment was from 50-80 years of age.

Was it applied in order to make patients no longer remember who they were, and where they were from? Or to forget history in general, including any recent change or catastrophe that may have occurred?

I think it worth noting too, how this time period roughly corresponds with the Soviet Gulag system, the network of forced labour camps that opened in 1918, and reached its peak during Joseph Stalin's rule from the 1930s to the early 1950s.

Once again, over this period millions of folk were interred by their own government and sentenced to hard labour for the most obscure and pettiest of reasons. According to Wikipedia;

> The emergent consensus among scholars is that, of the 14 million prisoners who passed through the Gulag camps and the 4 million prisoners who passed through the Gulag colonies from 1930 to 1953, roughly 1.5 to 1.7 million prisoners perished there or died soon after their release.

A mere fraction when compared to the estimated seven million Ukrainians, predominantly Christian, who were deliberately starved to death during the man-made famine known as the Holodomor, from 1932-1933.

This demographic also includes the orphan train movement and the foundling generation, who were most likely born in the 1850s to 1880s. Most researchers agree, that it's almost impossible to do justice to the number of orphans there actually were during this period. The true number they say, did not even enter the record books.

It's been noted that two conflicting themes run though Dickens novels and 19th century literature in general. That of marriage and female chastity. And that of orphans and adoption. The hundreds of thousands of orphans in the nineteenth century, is barely believable. Were women at the time really that promiscuous and care-free? Again, the narrative is not convincing. In fact, it's highly disturbing.

Why do we see so many late nineteenth century photographs of young children in workhouses using machinery that was obviously created for adult use? Were there not enough adults at the time to carry out this work?

Could it be that millions of babies and young children were forcibly taken from their parents, who in turn, were committed to spend the rest of their lives in Lunatic Asylums?

This stolen generation were then shipped around the world in order to repopulate other parts of the earth? Awaiting their arrival, were permanent amusement parks, with incubators and sanatoriums where folk could adopt a baby or infant?

All highly speculative of course, and none of which can be proven either way. Nevertheless, no official explanation is given for all the photographic evidence of virtually deserted cities. Nor for the vast amounts of mud we see in the streets, and the entire lower level of buildings being excavated from the soil.

Nevertheless, please don't fall for all the lies, the propaganda and deception. Historians and so-called Fact-Checkers, have been hired by the controllers and are paid good money, to obscure the horrible fact that the people ultimately responsible for the atrocities of Auschwitz, the Gulag, the Holodomor, and Hiroshima, still run the world today.

They are the ones responsible for the two world wars, 9-11, the Gulf Wars, the current war in the Ukraine, the ongoing, engineered Coveed-crisis, the energy crisis, the food crisis, and the worldwide shot-in-the-arm-for-billions agenda.

The Dark Age

The period of European history extending from about 500 AD to 1400–1500 AD, is traditionally known as the Middle Ages. Thus a period of somewhere between nine hundred, and one thousand years.

The "Dark Ages" is a term for the Middle Ages in Western Europe after the fall of the Western Roman Empire in 476 AD.

The concept came to characterize the entire Middle Ages as a time of intellectual darkness in Europe between the fall of Rome in 476AD and the Renaissance, generally placed around the beginning of the fourteenth century. Thus a period of approximately 920 years.

European historians traditionally date the beginning of the Age of Enlightenment with the death of Louis XIV of France in 1715.

Many historians now date the end of the Enlightenment Age as the start of the nineteenth century, with the latest proposed year being the death of Immanuel Kant in 1804. Again this would roughly correspond with the time period Napoleon conquered half of Europe. In all likelihood a fabricated cover story used to disguise a major cataclysmic event.

Although Jesuit, Luis de Alcasar's, systematic preterist exposition of prophecy was published in the sixteenth century, it should also be noted that the church of Rome, has been largely responsible for promoting the futurist interpretation of end-times prophecy.

It's also generally acknowledged, that John Nelson Darby first proposed and popularized the dispensationalist, pre-tribulation rapture in 1827. He advocated for a strong distinction between Israel and the church, and also popularized the idea that the church would be raptured or snatched to heaven just prior to the seventieth-week of Daniel.

Yet Daniel's seventy weeks of years, namely, 70x7=490 years, was perfectly fulfilled, when Jesus started his public ministry.

This is why there was an air of expectation and excitement in Israel at the time, for the religious Jews rightly understood that Daniel's prophetic seventy weeks, were almost at the point of conclusion.

Although in prison at the time, but having heard about all of the miracles being performed by Jesus, it was for this very reason that John the baptist, sent two of his disciples to ask Jesus;

"Art thou he that should come, or do we look for another?" *(Matthew 11:3.)* And why all the prophets and the law prophesied until John. *(Matthew 11:13.)*

Nevertheless, the historicist view of the past-fulfilment of prophecy was by and large dismissed, and Darby's futurist view of the end-times, was quickly accepted among many other Plymouth Brethren movements throughout England. It wasn't long before the doctrine of the pre-tribulation rapture had impacted American Christianity, primarily through their writings.

Popular books also contributed to acceptance of the pre-tribulation rapture, including William E. Blackstone's book "Jesus is Coming", published in 1878, which sold more than 1.3 million copies, and the Schofield Reference Bible, published in 1909 and 1919 and revised in 1967.

According to the gospel coalition website;

> The rise in popularity of Dispensationalism also occurred through Bible conferences, the rise of Bible institutes and colleges, the influence of Dallas Theological Seminary, and the popularity of radio and television programs from dispensational teachers. Hal Lindsey's book, *The Late Great Planet Earth*, and the *Left Behind* book series (Tim LaHaye and Jerry Jenkins) were books published from a dispensational perspective that became best sellers. Dispensationalism remains popular in the United States but also has many critics.

Dispensationalism is strongly connected to futurism, which in turn, generated a whole array of different rapture charts, predictors, and date-setters.

Yet, what if the generation who Jesus addressed more than 2,000 years ago, had witnessed his coming in the clouds, just as he assured them they would? Strictly speaking, any doctrine concerning the timing of the rapture would have little or no relevance today.

Why do our history books record the period of somewhere between nine hundred, and one thousand years, that followed the fall of the Roman empire, as being the Dark Age?

What if the timeline has been inverted? What if the Dark Age was actually the true Age of Enlightenment? History books tell us that beginning in 1685, humanity transitioned from the 'Dark Age' into the 'Age of Enlightenment', which ended in 1815.

Writes Michelle Gibson;

> What if the timeline we have been taught about in school, actually starts in the mid 1800's with a new false historic narrative superimposed onto the old world infrastructure? One which brought cruelty, great suffering, degradation and division to humanity?

What if it slowly began to dawn on millions of people worldwide, that the world they inhabited had plunged into an age of darkness? What if folk had started to recognize the past fulfilment of certain end-time prophecy from reading the Scriptures? What if these people began to share their concerns?

What if these people were labelled delusional, religious enthusiasts, and declared insane by the controllers, and committed to a Lunatic Asylum?

What if their babies and young children were taken from these people against their will, to repopulate other locations across the world?

Yes, I know, that's a lot of "what ifs". But no reasonable explanation is given for the worldwide explosion of mental health problems, the millions of orphans who appeared on the scene, nor for the tens of millions of folk who migrated to other countries, over more or less the same time period.

What if there were a common denominator?

Earlier I suggested the controllers may have had a two-fold agenda for instigating the two world wars.

1: To introduce the false ideology of Zionism, and to create the modern-day state of Israel, for the ultimate purpose of falsifying Biblical end-times prophecy as if it had never yet happened. And by following the blueprint of Scripture to do so.

2: For the purpose of destroying any physical evidence left behind, which might indicate the past fulfilment of Biblical prophecy.

Not only has world history been hidden or disguised, but by following the blueprint of scripture, the controllers intend to falsify end-time prophecy, as if it had never yet been fulfilled.

This deception will likely include the arrival of a false prophet, a false messiah and a fake rapture, courtesy of 'Project Blue Beam'.

America's links with Israel are there for all to see, and America was intentionally created to be destroyed. The pre-planned destruction of America will become the Scapegoat for "Babylon the great is fallen, is fallen", *(Revelation 18:2)* and out of her ashes, the phoenix will rise as their new world order.

Yet from a historicist viewpoint, this prophecy was fulfilled over 2,000 years ago with the fall of Babylon aka Jerusalem. This would have been coincident with the battle of Armageddon *(Revelation 18:16)* which most Christians believe is on the horizon.

On the other hand, Zionist Rabbis anticipate the War of Gog and Magog. They are most likely right, but for all the wrong reasons. For their expectations are based upon Ezekiel's prophecies in the Old Testament. Not on John's prophecy in the New Testament, which says Gog and Magog takes place *after* the millennial reign of Christ, and *after* the Little Season.

****

In the Introduction, I mentioned that the main theme of this book, should be considered a theory; an hypothesis. Multiple theories in fact, and an attempt to join the dots and tie them all altogether.

For it cannot be proven that scores of eleventh century peasants, with a modest collection of hand tools, were *not* responsible for the construction of all the massive cathedrals in England, back in the horse and cart era. Neither can it be proven that these magnificent structures were artistically crafted by unknown builders, with such finesse in order to perform a function.

Likewise, it cannot be proven that these huge buildings have been inherited in more recent times. Nor that thousands of old world buildings were displayed to the public at the World Fairs, under the guise of being temporary structures, in order to justify their destruction. Whilst there is a sound case for the timeline deception theory, once again it cannot be proven.

My purpose for writing this book, is to present these theories in a way that not only makes some sort of sense, but also as food for thought. I hope I've been able to achieve this.

Some will likely think, yes, it actually does make some sort of sense, whilst many, maybe the majority, will reject it all completely.

But each must draw their own conclusion.

From a Biblical perspective everything depends upon whether or not we read and believe the words of Jesus. That some of the generation whom he addressed a little over 2,000 years ago, witnessed His coming in the clouds, as he assured them they would.

For if we were to believe so, then we have little choice but to believe that the prophesied one thousand year reign has also been fulfilled. In which case, we have all been well and truly deceived. For in all likelihood, we are currently living in "The Little Season", a time of great deception and evil.

A realization of such enormity may well stir up feelings of bitterness and great disappointment, but should we really be surprised? For there can be no doubt whatsoever that we live in unprecedented times. A world that consists of layer upon layer of deceit and lies. That "thing" that masquerades as the UK Government, is an utter and total disgrace, which can now only be described as evil.

Everything that is going on is all by design of the World Economic Forum New World Order, to create a one world socialist Nazi government. Mainstream media is being used to promote their propaganda to brainwash the public and to keep people in a constant state of confusion and distraction while they pull off the greatest deception in history. By falsifying end times prophecy, as if it had not yet been fulfilled.

Let me be honest. For I would genuinely like to believe that when Jesus assured "this generation", that some would still be alive at his coming, he was *not* referring to those around him at the time, but rather to a distant and future generation. Our generation maybe. For if that were the case, the first resurrection, the rapture of believers in Christ, and the thousand year reign are still to come.

However, as previously discussed, in view of the multiple verses in the Scriptures which indicate the past fulfilment of much end times prophecy, it's more of a wishful thought, and one that is extremely hard to defend.

For when we read the New Testament with a different mindset, it becomes quite evident that the generation Jesus directly addressed, had witnessed him coming in the clouds as the Son of man, likely coincident with the fall of Babylon, aka Jerusalem.

Yet whether or not the millennial reign of Jesus Christ has already occurred, one thing is certain. A day of reckoning is coming, but it will come at a cost that most can't even begin to imagine.

For if we are living in the "little season", then the final rebellion against Jesus Christ, and the war of Gog and Magog *(Revelation 20:8)* is approaching at breakneck speed. If indeed we have all been born into the time period known as the 'Little Season', what then, should those who genuinely believe that Jesus is Lord, expect?

Good News

Every individual who enters this world, does so via the portal of the womb, and is born of water when mother's waters break. And every individual, is born subject to "the law of sin and death", from which, only "the law of the Spirit of life in Christ Jesus", can set a man free. *(Romans 8:2.)*

Which is precisely why Jesus stressed the need to be born again. Not of water (the womb) again, as Nicodemus once supposed, but this time born of the Spirit of God. For it is not the flesh of man that is born again, but the spirit of man. *(John 3:6.)*

Whilst confession is vocalized via the mouth, it is actually the spirit that confesses that Jesus Christ came in the flesh. And that spirit is of God, because it is born again, or born of God. *(1 John 5:1.)*

The *only* gospel or good news, by which men are saved, is the gospel of Jesus Christ, which is an *Everlasting* Gospel. *(Revelation 14:6.)* The *only* name given under heaven among men for salvation, is the name of Jesus. For there is no other name. *(Acts 4:12.)*

The name by which those partakers of the *first* resurrection were saved, is exactly the same name by which you and I are saved today. For there is no other. When Jesus prayed to the Father for the early believers, he also prayed for every future individual, who would come to believe in Him, due to the witness of those same early believers. The twelve disciples, the first evangelists and those who penned the four gospels. (*John 17:20-21.*)

Neither pray I for these alone, but for them also which shall believe on me through their word; That they all may be one; as thou, Father, art in me, and I in thee, that they also may be one in us: that the world may believe that thou hast sent me.

Whether or not there is a second rapture to come, we are not told. A *first* resurrection however, demands a second at least. We are told that "the rest of the dead lived not again until the thousand years were finished." *(Revelation 20:5.)*

Personally, I think "the rest of the dead" being raised, occurs after the final war of Gog and Magog, at the resurrection of the dead, to stand at the Final Judgement before the great white throne. *(Revelation 20:11.)*

Here, books (*plural*) are opened, plus another book, which is the book of life. And the dead were judged out of those things which were written in the books, according to their **works**. *(Revelation 20:12.)*

On the one hand, it is **not** possible to be saved by **works**. Yet, on the other hand, salvation unto everlasting life, is **not** possible without first doing the **works** of God.

John 6:29. Jesus answered and said unto them, This is the **work** of God, that ye believe on him whom he hath sent.

We are told that the heaven and the earth fled away from the face of him who sits on the great white throne. And no place was found for them. *(Revelation 20:11.)*

This, I believe, corresponds with "the day of the Lord", the day which comes "as a thief in the night", the day in which, "the heavens, being on fire, dissolve", and "the elements melt with fervent heat". *(2 Peter 3:10-12.)*

Indeed, I would imagine that when the entire physical realm is burned out of existence, all that remains, is the "Lake of Fire."

2 Peter 3:13. Nevertheless we, according to his promise, look for **new** heavens and a **new** earth, wherein dwelleth righteousness.

Revelation 21:1. And I saw a **new** heaven and a **new** earth: for the **first** heaven and the **first** earth were passed away; and there was no more sea.

Revelation 21:2. And I John saw the holy city, new Jerusalem, coming down from God out of heaven, prepared as a bride adorned for her husband.

1 Corinthians 2:9. But as it is written, Eye hath not seen, nor ear heard, neither have entered into the heart of man, the things which God hath prepared for them that love him.

1 John 5:2. By this we know that we love the children of God, when we love God, and keep his commandments.

1 John 3:23. And this is his commandment, That we should believe on the name of his Son Jesus Christ, and love one another, as he gave us commandment.

What does it mean to believe on the name of Jesus Christ? Everything! For the difference between belief and unbelief will determine one's eternal destiny. All men will die, for such is inevitable. Beyond which lies the judgement. Some men will die in their sins and meet God, the most Terrible and Righteous Judge. Others will meet God, the Father, who judges No Man. *(John 5:22 .)* Jesus said; "No man cometh unto the Father, but by me." *(John*

14:6) and "He that believeth on me hath everlasting life." *(John 6:47.)*

"For this is my blood of the new testament, which is shed for many for the remission of sins." *(Matthew 26:28.)*

Those who believe that Jesus is Lord can also believe;

Colossians 1:14. In whom we have redemption through his blood, even the forgiveness of sins:

1 Corinthians 6:20. For ye are bought with a price: therefore glorify God in your body, and in your spirit, which are God's.

Yet Jesus also said;

"I said therefore unto you, that ye shall die in your sins: for if ye ***believe not*** *that* I am he, ye shall die in your sins". *(John 8:24.)*

I'm not sure about you the reader, but personally, I cannot even begin to imagine the utter misery and the depth of despair experienced by those who die in their sins. Especially if aware that the forgiveness of sin unto eternal life had always been freely available to them, in the world from which they had recently departed.

Choose your Saviour Wisely.

And in the meanwhile, how does the thief on the cross fit into your thinking and theology?

No baptism, no communion, no confirmation, no speaking in tongues, no mission trip, no volunteer-ism, and no church clothes. He couldn't even bend his knees to pray. He didn't say the sinner's prayer and among other things, he was a thief.

Jesus didn't, take away his pain, heal his body, or smite the scoffers. Yet it was a thief who walked into paradise the same hour as Jesus, simply by believing. He had nothing more to offer other than his belief that Jesus was exactly who he said he was.

No spin, or clever sermons from brilliant theologians. No ego or arrogance, no skinny jeans, or crafty words. No shiny lights or burning candles, no soft piped-music or rock band playing, no doughnuts, biscuits or tea and coffee in the foyer.

Just a naked dying man on a cross, unable to even fold his hands to pray. All he could do was believe that Jesus was exactly who he claimed he was. And for this, the thief received the promise.

Choose your Saviour Wisely.

Printed in Great Britain
by Amazon

26129694R00116